PRAISE FOR *PEACE FR*

"This book is medicine for our time. It reminds us what we seem to have lost or been robbed of—that we are connected, that we belong, that the peace we hope to cultivate internally and externally have everything to do with each other. Hala artfully explores how embodying our interconnectedness—between our own physical, emotional, spiritual, and mental bodies, as well as between ourselves and others—creates the foundation of well-being and intrinsic interdependence that not only enables us to survive anxiety or despair but actually thrive in spite of it."
—Tessa Hicks Peterson, PhD, Pitzer College

"With a deep commitment to compassion and an avoidance of magical thinking, Hala Khouri promotes a culture of care by encouraging a global heart, critical consciousness, and active hope. The book offers a profound prescription for living with more reflection, peace, and connection in a world under threat." —Helene Shulman Lorenz, PhD, Pacifica Graduate Institute, author of *Toward Psychologies of Liberation*

"An accessible, engaging, and practical guide to healing from anxiety, both individually and collectively. Drawing on relatable stories from her own life, yoga teaching, and therapeutic experience, Hala Khouri offers practical insight into bringing ourselves back into regulation and living a more grounded life. I have learned so much from Hala and use these practices all the time! This book situates anxiety in the context of structural inequalities and social justice, showing us how inner peace is intimately intertwined with an outer world of justice and peace. It reminds us that we heal in connection with one another and offers us ways of doing so. This book offers much-needed somatic healing tools for our turbulent times." —Beth Berila, PhD, St. Cloud State University

"I have worked alongside Hala for well over fifteen years and know her to be highly intelligent, powerfully articulate, warm and inviting, and nuanced in her understanding of trauma and its many layered causes. This book is a breath of fresh air and exactly the kind of accessible and effective tool we all need in these times of change and crisis. I am confident that it will welcome, inspire, and support you in your journey to peace." —Suzanne Sterling, Voice of Change, cofounder of Off the Mat, Into the World

"Hala Khouri, the cofounder of Off the Mat, Into the World, has generously gathered her considerable wisdom in this book, indissolubly linking self-care with collective care. As we uncover how our personal anxieties and fears intermingle with those for our global neighbors and the natural world, Khouri tutors us on how to calm the nervous system and cultivate our relationship with suffering so that we can see and act with greater clarity." —Mary Watkins, PhD, author of *Mutual Accompaniment and the Creation of the Commons*

"Hala Khouri generously guides her reader to process their own internalized suffering, provides tools for self-regulation and reflection, invites critical thinking, and carves out a healing pathway toward collective care that can unite this world into peace. I'm so grateful for this powerful resource and will use it both in my personal healing practice and my public facilitation as a yoga teacher." —Seane Corn, author of *Revolution of the Soul*, cofounder of Off the Mat, Into the World

"It's hard to imagine any better time to have a thoughtful, straightforward book that directs us into deeper relationship with our selves. *Peace from Anxiety* doesn't bypass what incites us to be anxious personally and collectively, but it also doesn't leave us stuck with information overload. Hala Khouri balances context, examples, and relatable stories with reaffirming, down-to-earth practices that bring us back home to the bodies we all yearn to be comfortable in. There's something for anyone who wants to learn in this tender guide."—Rev. angel Kyodo williams, coauthor of *Radical Dharma: Talking Race, Love, and Liberation*

PEACE
from
ANXIETY

Get Grounded, Build Resilience, and
Stay Connected Amidst the Chaos

Hala Khouri

SHAMBHALA

Shambhala Publications, Inc.
2129 13th Street
Boulder, Colorado 80302
www.shambhala.com

Note: This book is not meant to replace the diagnosis or treatment of
anxiety by a qualified mental health provider. Please consult a health-care
professional if you are unable to manage or feel you need support.

Cover art: Igor Vitkovskiy / Shutterstock
Cover design: Kate E. White
Interior design: Greta D. Sibley

9 8 7 6 5 4 3 2

Printed in the United States of America

⊗ This edition is printed on acid-free paper that meets the
American National Standards Institute z39.48 Standard.
♻ This book is printed on 30% postconsumer recycled paper.
For more information please visit www.shambhala.com.
Shambhala Publications is distributed worldwide by
Penguin Random House, Inc., and its subsidiaries.

Library of Congress Cataloging-in-Publication Data
Names: Khouri, Hala, author.
Title: Peace from anxiety: get grounded, build resilience, and
stay connected amidst the chaos / Hala Khouri.
Description: Boulder, Colorado: Shambhala Publications, Inc., [2021] |
Includes bibliographical references and index.
Identifiers: LCCN 2020029111 | ISBN 9781611808100 (trade paperback)
Subjects: LCSH: Anxiety. | Stress (Psychology) | Stress management.
Classification: LCC BF575.A6 K55 2021 | DDC 152.4/6—dc23
LC record available at https://lccn.loc.gov/2020029111

I dedicate this book to my mom,
Dalal Ghorra Khouri
(June 2, 1945–February 9, 2020).
You taught me how to love big and include the
world in my heart. Thank you. I miss you.

CONTENTS

INTRODUCTION

Anxiety and These Overwhelming Times

THIS BOOK IS about stress, anxiety, overwhelm . . . whatever word you use to describe your suffering or the suffering of those around you—your children, loved ones, colleagues, or even strangers. More importantly, this book is about hope, resilience, reclamation, and healing. At my core, I'm an optimist. I believe that people are inherently good, and that we all ultimately want to feel safe, connected, loved, and happy. We want our lives to be meaningful. Yet research suggests that anxiety is on the rise, with more than forty million people in the US—and millions more around the world—experiencing anxiety each year.[1] Polls show that more people feel anxious—not just about their own personal lives, but also about larger issues ranging from politics to climate change.[2] As you'll see in this book, while some anxiety can be healthy, unmanaged anxiety can negatively impact every aspect of our lives—from our mental health and physical health to our relationships. Unhappiness is an epidemic, and many of us have lost the roadmap to well-being.

Being well is not necessarily simple for many people, especially when there's so much that's out of our control. While we can't always control or change the things in life that cause us anxiety, we do have some control over our response to these challenges. By better understanding the dimensions of our anxiety—both internal and external—and by getting some tools to work with how we react, we can find more peace. Also, when we can contextualize our anxiety in relation to factors like race, class, gender, and current and historical events, it can offer us a perspective that goes beyond mainstream mental health models that focus just on our personal and interpersonal issues. This peace we seek can expand beyond our own well-being into a vision of a peace-filled world.

Anxiety

The *Oxford English Dictionary* defines anxiety as "a feeling of worry, nervousness, or unease, typically about an imminent event or something with an uncertain outcome." Anxiety is experienced differently by different people, and even our own experience with it can vary at different points in our lives. Sometimes our anxiety is alerting us to something real that needs to be addressed. In that case, it is an accurate assessment and a reliable guide. Sometimes our anxiety is misleading us or is a reaction to something that is actually not there. Much of the time, it's something in between. Some of us experience debilitating anxiety that impacts our capacity to function and live a full life. Some of us have a diagnosed anxiety disorder or other mental health issues. Some of us experience anxiety as a constant state that we have gotten so used to enduring that it has come to feel normal. Some of us don't even realize that we have anxiety, because it manifests as digestive issues, or headaches, or muscle and joint pain. (Anxiety can be an underlying contributor to these conditions and other health issues.) At the end of the day, anxiety sucks. Those of us who live with it often use a lot of energy and attention trying to manage it, anticipate it, or avoid it. This can cause us to avoid situations that we fear will trigger our anxiety, which can make our world smaller and smaller. For many people, once we've experienced unmanageable anxiety, we become preoccupied with the fear that it will come back—and that makes us even more anxious!

In this book I'm going to take you on a journey to transform your relationship with anxiety so you can move through life's challenges with more ease and open up to authentic joy and meaning in your life. This isn't about getting rid of anxiety completely (that's not always possible); it's about changing your relationship with it so it doesn't rule your life. When we are trying to get away from our anxiety, life is exhausting. It's like trying to pull your fingers out of a Chinese finger trap toy: the harder you pull, the tighter it gets. You can only be free of the trap when you stop resisting it. This is how you're going to stop being overwhelmed by your anxiety—by not resisting it. This process requires radical self-exploration to uncover some of the root causes of your anxiety (*radical* means "root") in order to make a permanent shift. In addition to this deep work, I'll share tools that can offer some more immediate relief as well. You could just use the quick tools to manage your anxiety and stop there, but if you want to take your healing to the next level so you can find freedom rather than just managing your anxiety, take the deep dive and read the whole book. You won't regret it. You deserve peace. I wholeheartedly believe that it is human nature to feel happy and free, and I've dedicated my life and work to helping to create a world where everyone has this opportunity.

Ultimately this book is about integration—accepting and embracing the lost parts of ourselves, the parts we've been told are not okay, and the parts we are afraid of. This book is about finding a pathway back to ourselves, our community, and the whole world. Well-being is not an individual state; we are part of an interdependent web of life. This concept exists in many cultures, both ancient and current, yet many of us have lost touch with it, especially those of us in Westernized cultures. The myth of individual wellness is being revealed; this is part of the chaos we're experiencing on a collective global level. We cannot be truly well on our own. We need to figure out how we can all be well together. This book will take us on a journey from individual well-being to *collective liberation*, a term that many leaders in today's social justice movements use to point to a reality where all beings are free—physically, mentally, and emotionally. Collective liberation is about a world where no person is subordinate to another, where everyone is treated with dignity and respect, and where our understanding of interconnectedness teaches us that no one is fully well unless everyone is well. It's ambitious, I know, but join me and let's figure out how we can all be well together.

Who Is This Book For?

Some of us feel more burdened by personal challenges than what is happening globally. This book is for you. Some of us feel the weight of the world's issues on our shoulders and minimize our personal well-being because we are in the trenches supporting others. This book is for you. Some of us have been beaten down by the world and need a sanctuary where we can heal. This book is for you too.

This book is about healing your body, mind, and soul. By body I mean your nervous system and your ability to self-regulate, by mind I mean your thoughts and habitual belief patterns, and by soul I mean that part of you that makes meaning of the world, of suffering, and of who you are in the face of that. I hope you'll find insights that will resonate and light you up, but to truly transform your suffering, you'll need to put in the work. Don't rush through this book. Maybe read one section and wait a few days before you go on to the next. Let the ideas sink in, not just the ones you love but the ones you hate—especially the ones you hate, because they can probably take you to that uncomfortable place where healing often occurs. Use a journal and take some time to answer the reflection questions. Try the practices. This work is messy and uplifting. It's uncomfortable and liberating. It's worth it. What's the alternative? To stay safely stuck and unhappy?

My Own Peace with Anxiety

I write this book drawing not only on my professional experience in somatic counseling supporting people with trauma and anxiety, but also my own personal experience. I've been studying psychology and human development since middle school. My undergraduate degree is in psychology and religion, and I have master's degrees in counseling psychology and in community psychology. I'm also trained in Somatic Experiencing, a body-based trauma therapy. I've been teaching trauma-informed yoga and working in private practice with trauma survivors for more than a decade. I've also spent a lot of time working with nonprofits doing community healing work. I've worked with domestic violence shelters, gang interventionists, incarcerated people, social workers, and artists who tell stories about trauma and injustice. In 2006 I cofounded a nonprofit organization called Off the Mat, Into the World. We train people who want to be leaders in their community using a model grounded in embodied practices like yoga and meditation to foster self-awareness and accountability. Over the past two decades I have trained or worked with thousands of people who are either healing from their own trauma and anxiety or who are leaders wanting to do healing work in the world. Their perspectives and wisdom have shaped my work profoundly.

It is also important that I share part of my personal story with you, for this has also shaped my approach. Our thoughts are shaped by our life experiences; what we can and can't see is determined by these experiences as well. I do my best to include the experience of others when I write, but I am inevitably limited by my own life experience.

I was born in Beirut, Lebanon, in 1973, two years before the Lebanese Civil War broke out. One year into the war, we were able to leave—my mother, father, little sister, and I made our way to Middlesborough, Kentucky, where my father had secured a job for a year. Eventually we landed in Miami, Florida, to be near family. My mom used to tell us that in America, the houses were made of chocolate. We were excited to leave, and ready to be far from the violence and instability of the war—and for the chocolate. Modern-day Lebanon is fraught with a history of internal conflict and violence in a region impacted by centuries of colonization and occupation, the latter of which still exists today. The Lebanese Civil War, a violent and destructive period of seventeen years, officially ended in 1990, but many argue the war hasn't ended. Its effects continue to mark the country, its people, and the diaspora caused by the violence and instability in a significant way. It's no surprise that I dedicated my life to understanding trauma. There's a little girl in me that wants everyone to heal so that they can stop fighting and just get along.

As a child, growing up in Miami, a multicultural city in the United States, I never personally experienced any bias or discrimination for being Arab. Pre-9/11 the stereotype of the "Arab terrorist" was less ubiquitous and my family was educated and had class privilege that connected us with other professionals and let us feel a level of acceptance in a culture that wasn't ours. We did tend to socialize with other Lebanese people for the most part, and as I look back, we had very few friends who were from the United States. We managed to build a community of other immigrants, which buffered us from the feeling of being "other."

Coming to the US was not easy for my parents, especially my mother. She didn't speak English, and she had her own struggles with my father. By middle school, I found myself in the role of confidant to my mom and mediator between my parents. In seventh grade I knew I wanted to study psychology—I had a burning desire to understand how people work. I think I hoped that if I could figure out my dad, I could explain him to my mom, and then she'd be happy. Starting at the age of twelve, I devoured self-help books and then I would try to coach my mom so that she could feel happier and more empowered.

By age fourteen, I became enraged and filled with concern for my mom and frustration with our household roles. My father worked during the day, and my mom was in charge of the house and children twenty-four seven. What I saw was my mother cooking and cleaning all the time while my dad sat on the couch watching TV and drinking whenever he was home. He never contributed to the domestic activities; it was taken for granted that those were solely my mother's responsibility. It felt unfair to me, yet we all put up with it. One day I decided to speak up. My mother reprimanded me, and my father didn't speak to me for a week. When I realized that I couldn't express my anger at home, I turned it outward. I declared that I was a feminist. I had no idea what this word meant, but I had a burning sense of injustice inside of me that wanted to be expressed.

In college my cause became vegetarianism, animal rights, and the environment. When I went home for the holidays, I told my family they were animal murderers when they ate meat, and I made them watch videos about factory farming to try and convince them to change their evil ways. I was very unpleasant to be around. When I look back, if I'm totally honest with myself, I can see that part of me loved it when other people were "wrong" so I could feel self-righteous and "right." I always had a cause that let me point fingers at everyone else, and for a long time, I refused to notice the three fingers pointing back at me each time I did that. I hadn't yet connected my inner workings with how I approached the outer world. It was much easier to blame others for my feelings—*they* were animal killers, *they* were ignorant, *they* were immoral and bad.

By constantly being disappointed with the world and making it my job to fix it, I was avoiding my own grief and vulnerability. But in quiet moments when there were no distractions, the feelings would surface. They were intolerable, so I numbed out with chocolate and sugar. It was a tumultuous existence. By day, I was dedicated to important causes, being a good friend, and succeeding in school; by night I sat in bed devouring jars of Nutella chocolate spread, plagued by shame. I felt like I was performing my life—everyone saw me as a passionate and happy person but inside of me was a darkness that I hid diligently. I focused on taking care of others. I was a confidant for all of my friends, a peer counselor in high school, and a crisis counselor in college. I figured if I was helping others with their struggles, I wouldn't have to feel mine. That strategy only goes so far; there isn't enough chocolate in the world to keep it up.

After I graduated from college I finally began my journey of looking inward, for real, to expose and shine light on the parts of myself that were running the show unconsciously. I did group therapy and individual therapy and read more self-help books—but this time with the intention of healing myself, not my mom or everyone around me. I signed up for every workshop on healing I could afford, I traveled, I sat with shamans in the jungle, I got a master's degree in psychology, I became a yoga teacher, and I worked really hard at improving myself in every possible way. At one point my sister said to me, "You need to stop self-improving." She was right. At some point my obsession with fixing myself had become my new way to not actually have to be present with myself as I was. I had replaced numbing out with sugar with magical thinking, self-help workshops, and detox diets. Those pesky defenses! They will come back dressed up in different outfits if we're not careful.

In my early thirties I achieved a sense of balance and well-being I'd never thought possible; I'd wake up in the morning amazed that I wasn't eaten up with struggle and shame. This didn't happen overnight. It's not like I finally found "the answer." It was a process that happened so slowly, in the subterrane of my being, that I didn't realize it fully until the moment I did. One thing I learned through obsessively seeking a quick fix to my problems is that there's no such thing. Anyone selling you that is a charlatan. Healing is slow. When change happens really quickly, it rarely lasts. Both research and experience suggest that slow healing—deep and sustainable—is what lasts.

When I was thirty-two, I married my second husband, Paul. Yes, there was a first husband, my "practice husband," as I like to call him. He was my high school sweetheart; we were together for twelve years. That relationship taught me so much and helped me unwind from a lot of my unhealthy patterns. He was a safer person to work that stuff out with than my dad. I think that relationships (romantic or platonic) quicken our healing because they are mirrors for us. So by the time I found Paul, I had worked through a ton of my issues and, at forty-two, he had as well. This second relationship felt easy and light. We weren't bogged down by lots of unconscious patterns. Then we had kids.

If you think you have your shit together, have a kid or two and that illusion will quickly be shattered. For me, having children exposed (and continues to expose) more layers of beauty and muck inside of me than I ever thought I had. I'm raising two rambunctious boys. They bring out the best and the worst in me. I often say that parenting is the most empowering and humiliating journey. At least that's what it's been for me.

Around the age of forty-one (when my kids were four and seven) I began experiencing anxiety for the first time in my life. I had experienced fear and worry before, but this was different. This feeling preoccupied me and started to color almost everything I did. It took me almost a year to realize what was happening. It started with developing a fear of flying. Monthly flights for work, which used to feel like peaceful breaks from the chaos of life, suddenly felt extremely dangerous and precarious, and every sound and movement was indicative of immanent disaster. During flights, my hands would go numb, my heart would race, and everything felt loud and chaotic. Soon the anxiety would start a few days before flying. I was becoming anxious about getting anxious. I felt trapped!

After a while I started feeling anxious if I was a passenger in a car, or if one of my kids complained of feeling sick. The worst was when my anxiety would come up randomly with no particular trigger. One day I was driving my kids to school, and in the middle of making a left turn I started to have a panic attack. I worked so hard to manage it so that they wouldn't get scared, but I literally felt that I could black out at any moment. My anxiety had lots of flavors. Sometimes it was pure sensation: heart racing and constricted breathing for no obvious reason. Sometimes it was a feeling of doom and gloom, like something absolutely terrible was about to happen. I found myself in a constant negotiation with life, trying to anticipate what possible bad things could befall me and my family and what I could and could not handle. I was completely preoccupied with my anxiety. It was exhausting!

Given that so much of my life's work has been supporting people dealing with anxiety, I knew what I needed to do. I reached out to friends and loved ones, booked more therapy sessions, had a physical and got blood work done, made sure I was getting enough rest, and more. I was surprised by how many friends I spoke with also struggled with anxiety or went through periods of struggling with it. Many had never spoken to me about it; they suffered in secret. By being open about my struggles with friends (and even acquaintances), I knew I wasn't alone, and that helped a lot.

It took a few years of addressing my anxiety from several perspectives to find relief. I learned that anxiety, on a physical level, is often the first symptom of hormone changes for people approaching menopause—this was the case for me. Psychologically I had to confront the fact that I'd spent most of my life defending myself against vulnerability and fear, and now it was time to truly confront those feelings so I could move through them, rather than around them. Spiritually I had to find a way to include suffering as part of life without bypassing it.

I had to come to terms with the fact that terrible things can happen to anyone, even me, and I can still be okay even in the face of knowing that. I also had to find a way to not become overwhelmed by the knowledge that so many people on the planet are suffering. As I became more and more aware of my own privilege relative to the profound inequities that exist in the world (e.g., my class privilege, education privilege, and light-skinned privilege), I had to find ways to neither minimize any of this nor feel responsible for all the suffering in the world.

Working with anxiety has been part of my journey. I am not totally anxiety-free—of course it comes up once in a while—but I am no longer afraid of being anxious, and when I feel it I know I can cope with it. In fact, my capacity to feel a broad range of emotions is deeper and more rich now. I am able to be touched by life in a way I never was before, because I'm no longer defending against feeling too much. I can let my heart be broken by life and know that I will recover. I've also found that if I want to work toward justice for all beings and a world where everyone can be well, I need to be well. This allows me to commit more fully to my work and be more generous with my energy in order to uplift others. Being caught up in my own anxiety doesn't help all of the people marginalized and targeted by the world.

Healing and Social Justice

My path has taken me from a focus on personal healing to a focus on collective healing. There was a point in my journey early on where my obsession with my own well-being was separating me more and more from the world. I couldn't tolerate listening to the news with all its negativity and divisiveness. Plus, acknowledging the suffering of others didn't gel with my flawed "everything happens for a reason" paradigm. My diet was so specific I could barely go out to eat anywhere. My friends were all like me—they had similar values and worldviews. I judged anyone who didn't hold the same beliefs I did about the world. I was kind of a jerk, actually.

My focus changed when I began to understand more fully how trauma can be caused by culture and social systems—not just individuals—and how we each have different locations within these systems. Some of us are privileged by them, and some of us are harmed. Looking at individuals—our struggles and successes and failings—is only part of the picture. Teaching yoga to incarcerated youth in Los Angeles illustrated the power of these systems to me in the early 2000s. Many of the girls I taught were there on charges of prostitution. This was before sex trafficking laws changed and the law recognized that these children were *victims* of a crime, not perpetrators of it. How could I justify a belief that somehow the universe wanted these girls to have this experience? To be abused and then criminalized for it? I felt like I was part of the problem by coming in to teach them yoga in order to manage their emotions when they were completely justified in being angry and indignant. The healing practice felt like it could be harmful if it suggested they were to blame for their situation. Law enforcement and policies harmed these young women, and by not recognizing the serious flaws and biases in these systems, many people blamed the victims, rather than the larger systems at play. Yes, individual healing practices might be helpful in managing trauma, but they are incomplete and inadequate without addressing the broader systemic injustices that can traumatize so many. Recognizing the power of systems is important—to our path of personal healing and also to healing the pain we see in the world.

My own family is made up of people with different identities that tend to be targeted in the world—Muslim, gay, Black, Arab, and neurodivergent. My husband is Black and Jewish. My kids are Arab, Jewish, white, and Black. My family represents the future I want for our world, where differences are not tolerated but celebrated. A world where we can be together and not have to be the same. I believe that ultimately our suffering comes from separation. As we can feel more whole within ourselves, we can find that with each other. Happiness is connection.

Overview of the Book

This book is a journey from separation to connection on all levels. This is not a linear process, and you will certainly move through different emotions as we touch on different topics. We're going to look at what healing can look like on personal, interpersonal, and global levels. The personal level is about your own self-regulation and ability to feel good in your body and mind. I'll review the basics of how stress, anxiety, and trauma impact the nervous system and what specific tools and techniques can help us release anxiety and build resilience. The interpersonal level is about our connection to other people, our surroundings, and beyond. Feeling connected is vital to being well; when we cultivate and nurture these connections, we are held by a larger web of life and meaning. Finally, we will examine what it means to be a global citizen and contribute to a future of collective hope and optimism. This holistic view of anxiety is key for transforming our fear into peace and living a life dedicated to freedom and well-being for all.

So much of anxiety is a manifestation of our concern or doubt about our place in the world. This book will help you understand that you are a vital part of an ecosystem. As you understand your own psychology and physiology and how this ecosystem impacts you (and how you impact others) pathways to healing will be revealed. A collective care paradigm doesn't require us to be perfectly healed before we get to meaningfully participate in the world; it invites us all to show up exactly as we are, without shame, so we can hold each other and be held in this larger container. This allows all of us to be transformed for the better, so we can not only heal, but thrive.

PEACE FROM ANXIETY

Your Body Is Your GPS

Tools for Self-Regulation

OUR BODY IS our guidance system, sort of like the GPS that many cars, airplanes, and smartphones are equipped with for navigation. We are constantly taking in stimuli from the outside world and translating it into thoughts, sensations, and emotions, which fuel our actions. We are also responding to internal stimuli that color our view of the world. All of this information helps us make meaning of life and our place in it. This meaning making is also influenced by our history and ancestry, our relationship with suffering, the sociopolitical context we're in, and our spiritual beliefs (if we have them). Our first step in working with anxiety is understanding our body—how it's feeling, where these sensations come from, and how we can navigate these feelings. It's impossible to feel good if our nervous system is on high alert or shut down. In the next three chapters I'm going to break down what I mean by this and give you some practices to help tune and calibrate your personal navigation system—your body!

Over time I've learned to better identify anxiety in my body—perhaps you can relate. A few years ago, my husband, Paul, was told by his cardiologist that he needed a pacemaker to avoid having a stroke because his heart wasn't beating fast enough. The procedure went smoothly and, at his follow-up appointment, the doctor assured us that Paul's chances of having a stroke were now lowered to 1 percent. A few days after the appointment, we set off on a three-hour drive toward Three Rivers, California, a town where we had rented a house with a group of friends and their children for spring break. As our journey began, we were all in good spirits—our boys in the back were chatting about the trip and I was looking forward to being in nature with friends.

A few minutes into the drive, I noticed Paul touch his hand to his chest. I could have sworn he had a momentary look of concern on his face too. In less than a second, my whole body got hot, my heart started to race, my hands and legs began to tingle, and I felt panicked. Even though I had just been assured by the doctor that he was healthy and not at risk of a stroke, I felt like he was about to have one right there, driving all of us on the 405 freeway at 70 mph. I asked him how he was feeling, and he smiled and said, "great!" as he turned up the music on the radio.

Although my mind believed him, my body did not. Now that my internal alarm bells had been sounded, I found myself tracking his every move. From the corner of my eye, I noticed his breathing pattern, his facial expression, what he was doing with his arms—and all of it made me sure he was going to lose consciousness and we'd have a deadly car accident. I felt like I was in a movie scene where everyone is happy and carefree but the ominous music in the background lets you know that something really awful is about to happen. I was able to manage my fear until it was my turn to drive, at which point I felt much better.

That whole weekend was challenging for me. We were with eight children under the age of ten, and they were doing what kids do by a river—jumping off rocks, swimming, and climbing trees. Normally I love this stuff. I don't worry too much about kids getting hurt; in fact, it's good for them to get a bit bumped and bruised playing. But this time everything felt dangerous and precarious. The trees looked so tall and the rocks so jagged and ready to break open a child's head. I kept asking the adults around me if we should tell the kids to stop doing certain things because they were too risky. Most of the time they said no. While everyone else was relaxed and having fun, I was anxiously awaiting the impending doom one of our children was inevitably going to suffer at any moment.

That evening I was feeling irritated at one of my friends. I had no reason for it; she had done nothing wrong! In fact, everyone was kind of annoying me. I finally realized that my internal GPS was off. I was reading cues that weren't dangerous as alarm bells, and I didn't feel connected to the people around me. Things felt loud and chaotic. I wasn't trusting the flow of life. In fact, I was assuming the worst. My internal environment was such a stark contrast to my external environment, which was joyful and light.

Part of me just wanted to have a couple of glasses of wine and call it a day, but I knew that if I did that my discomfort would be numbed out for a few hours and come back with a vengeance the next day. Instead I decided to go sit by the river alone, away from any irritating friends or children about to maim themselves on a rock. I spent a few moments just acknowledging what I was feeling. I felt my tight chest and racing heart. I acknowledged that I felt anxious, scared, and out of control. I let myself feel the feelings in my body as I tried to also notice the beautiful environment I was in. I remember staring at the water running over the rocks, trying to feel the rhythm of that reassuring flow in my body. I was so used to feeling a sense of ease in my breath and a groundedness in my being that I took it for granted, and now that it was gone it was disorienting and scary. As I felt the ground beneath me, listened to the soothing sound of the river, and watched the water flow over the rocks, I felt a shift in my body, like a sense of remembering that things are okay and that I don't have to be looking out for danger all the time. I felt my breath come back to me and everything settled. It was a much-needed pause after forty-eight hours of being on high alert.

Self-Regulation

You might relate to the story above, or you might have even felt this way for most of your life—like your inner world doesn't gel with your outer world. Or you might feel that your outer world is actually so chaotic that your inner world reflects it and you can't find a moment of peace. As mentioned earlier, whether we realize it or not, our body (and more specifically, our nervous system), like a GPS, is our guidance system. When we're *regulated*, our body can guide us toward safety and pleasure and away from danger and pain. We can feel like life is generally safe (when it is), people are good, and things are fairly predictable. We can trust our gut feelings. But when our body is *dysregulated*, like mine was on that trip, we have a hard time knowing what is safe or dangerous, what to move away from and what to move toward. We don't know how to navigate the world around us because our guidance system is off and we can't trust it.

Sometimes we don't realize our GPS is off, and we believe what we feel is accurate. In this case, it can feel like life is conspiring to hurt us or like we have terrible luck all the time. We can feel like we're always ending up in the same situation and that we don't have the agency to make things better. When we're dysregulated, we may interpret our fear as an accurate assessment of a situation when it's not, or the opposite—we shut down and miss cues that tell us something is unsafe.

Regardless of whether our external environment is actually safe or not (for many people it's somewhere in between), we need an internal guidance system that we can rely on. Without it, life can feel overwhelming, and we can find ourselves feeling anxious and out of control at the slightest provocation. Understanding how to regulate ourselves is one of the most powerful ways to feel empowered and to manage our anxiety. This doesn't mean we always feel good; rather, it means that we feel that we can cope with life's challenges. When we're self-regulated we trust ourselves and we're able to take in the good stuff, let go of the bad, and experience what psychologist Mihaly Csikszentmihalyi calls "flow."[1]

Elements of Self-Regulation

On a physical level, being self-regulated consists of feeling *grounded*, *centered*, and *in present time*. When we are self-regulated, we're able to be with what we're experiencing without feeling overwhelmed. We feel that we have the internal resources to cope and respond to whatever may arise. When we're self-regulated, we are in a brain state that is responsive rather than reactive. We can trust our emotions to alert and guide us, and life feels manageable. On the other hand, when we are *dysregulated*, we are not able to manage what we are experiencing; this can make us feel anxious, depressed, manic, or even numb. We can feel out of control and can act impulsively and in a way that doesn't serve our best interests. When we're dysregulated, life can feel impossible to navigate.

Self-regulation is an embodied state, not an idea. We can often "know" something in our mind, such as, "it's probably not a good idea to yell at my boss right now," or "a little turbulence won't make the plane crash," and still act or feel completely otherwise. Just because our head knows something doesn't mean our body has gotten the memo. But when we're self-regulated, we can trust the signals of our body to guide us through the world and we can be discerning when our body may be triggered into a response that isn't ideal or accurate. We can notice our impulses and not act on them (such as yelling at our boss). We can also feel our fear without catastrophizing (such as being convinced that a plane is about to crash because of turbulence). When we're regulated we're able to recover from stressful events and find balance again.

Not all unpleasant feelings are signs of being dysregulated. Unpleasant feelings are important because they may be giving us important information. This is part of life, and when our GPS is running smoothly, we should be able to experience a variety of emotions. Our emotions and sensations help us navigate the world by alerting us to how we feel about things. They help us move toward what's good for us and away from what's not. Also, self-regulation is not synonymous with being physically healthy, young, fit, or pain-free. Someone generally considered physically healthy could feel dysregulated inside. Similarly, someone living with a short- or long-term illness could be regulated inside. (Although it's hard to be regulated when dealing with chronic pain, I've known people with serious illnesses who have found peace inside and are very grounded.)

There are some simple practices that can help us get regulated when we feel anxious, stressed, or just off balance. These are practices for building internal resources to support us so we can be grounded, centered, and present amidst whatever is going on. Finding a way to regulate our bodies and emotions can be one of the most important steps toward well-being. These simple practices can quickly move you from a state of nervous system arousal into a place of calm and ease. I encourage you to try them for yourself—either by putting the book down immediately after reading each one, or by planning a time in the near future to do them. Testing them out in your own body will help you learn which ones work best for you.

These practices can also change your brain. Research has found that the human brain is more malleable than previously thought.[2] *Neuroplasticity* is the ability of the brain to form new connections and pathways and change how its circuits are wired. Self-regulation practices help us build these new neural connections so that we literally rewire our brain and nervous system to increase our resilience and capacity to deal with stress without being overwhelmed.

Getting Grounded

There's a Chinese proverb that says, "When the roots are deep, there's no reason to fear the wind." This is the essence of grounding—feeling so solid and rooted in yourself that you don't have to resist anything. The opposite of this is when we feel unsupported and thus disoriented or spacey, like an uprooted plant flailing about in a storm. When we are grounded, we are resourced—we feel we have the capacity and tools to deal with what comes our way. We can feel grounded through our legs and feet or through any part of the body that is touching the ground, a floor, a chair, and so forth. We can even ground through our hands, and for people who use wheelchairs or crutches, grounding can happen through contact with mobility devices. The breath can also be something that grounds us and helps us feel more solid and stable.

GROUNDING PRACTICE 1

Find a comfortable seated position. Bring your attention to the parts of your body that are touching the floor, or the parts of your body that are touching something that touches the floor—for example, a chair or cushion. Notice these areas—perhaps your feet, back of thighs, bottom, arms, or hands. If your feet are on the floor, gently press them down and notice how your legs feel. Are they strong? Weak? Heavy? Light? Feel your seat bones on the chair, or your back against the chair. Allow your spine to lengthen the more you ground down, just like a tree that is able to rise to the sun as it deepens its roots. As you bring awareness to the places in your body that are being supported by the floor or chair, notice if anything settles in your body or just generally feels better.

GROUNDING PRACTICE 2

Cross your forearms in front of your body and squeeze your opposite arm with each hand. Gently squeeze your hands up the arms to your shoulders. Notice if anything settles in your body or your breath deepens and if there is a particular part of the movement that feels especially good.

GROUNDING PRACTICE 3

Stand with your feet a bit wider than hip-distance apart and your knees slightly bent, or you may sit, tuning in to your seat bones. Start to sway side to side. Notice the shift in weight in your feet (or seat bones) and how your legs feel. Tune in to your muscles and how they engage as you sway. Notice if anything settles in the rest of your body as you get more grounded in your lower body.

Getting grounded can help shift us out of a state of high nervous system arousal or shut down into a state of being settled and present. My friend Rafael once shared a story about the power of these tools in his own life. Rafael grew up in East Los Angeles in a neighborhood plagued by gang violence, racial profiling, and overpolicing. He also spent several years in foster care. He mostly managed to stay out of trouble but did get harassed by police and was sent to a juvenile detention center a few times for minor infractions. I invited Rafael on a retreat with me in Big Sur, California, one summer. During one of our sessions we learned grounding techniques for self-regulation. Rafael already had a meditation practice, but grounding was a new tool for him.

The next day Rafael and another participant left the retreat center and found a beach nearby to hang out on. The property owner found them and told them that he could send them to jail for trespassing on private property. Rafael said that when he heard the word "jail" coming from this man, his heart rate went up, his arms got hot, and he felt like he wanted to punch the man and run away. It's possible this affluent white beach owner was influenced by Rafael's skin color, which would not have been the first time Rafael was racially profiled. Though triggered, Rafael remembered the grounding prompt and focused on his feet on the ground and his breath. This helped him settle and, as he regained his composure, he made the conscious choice to reach out and shake the man's hand and apologize for trespassing rather than challenging him aggressively. When he did this, the man settled as well. Rafael felt empowered for being able to deescalate the situation and have some control over what happened.

Getting Centered

When we are centered, our sense of self and our center of power is inside of us, regardless of what is happening around us. We have a sense of personal agency and self-efficacy in our life. Although we may not be able to control everything that is happening around us, we are able to manage our own emotions and behavior. When our center is outside of us, we feel and experience that our safety and well-being is at the mercy of external forces; we may feel powerless and helpless. Sometimes it's actually true that our safety is in the hands of others, and this can be very stressful. In those situations, centering our attention on potential sources of danger is an appropriate response in an attempt to stay safe. However, when we are forced to endure circumstances where we have little control over our well-being or safety for a long time, it can be hard to cultivate a sense of center and recognize moments when we actually do have some agency.

Take Ellen, for example. Ellen came to me for therapy because she kept finding herself in relationships with people who were abusive, both physically and emotionally. She didn't know why she kept repeating this cycle. Given her history, this made sense. Ellen grew up with an alcoholic father who was very moody even when sober. He was very critical and could fly into a rage at any moment. The whole family was on guard around him, and when he drank, he became even more unpredictable. Ellen learned to cope with this by being hypervigilant around him and always tracking his mood and state of being. She could tell by his footsteps when he came home from work if he was in a bad mood and if this was going to be a night of heavy drinking. When he would start drinking, she would hide away in her room, reading books and listening to music. She knew that any interaction with him when he was drunk wouldn't end well, and she wanted to avoid that at all costs. Ellen was protective of her younger sister, who wasn't as skilled at assessing the situation and so would often find herself the object of her father's anger. In addition to avoiding his rage, Ellen learned that if she behaved and did well in school, it would make her dad happy. When he was pleased with her, he was less likely to take his anger out on her, so she made sure to share her academic accomplishments with him.

Ellen's attention was always centered on her father. In fact, the whole family system revolved around him and managing his anger and outbursts. This made sense because if Ellen could accurately assess how he was doing, she could usually ensure safety for herself and her sister. His state was more relevant to her well-being than her own state, so it served her to attune to him so intensely. As an adult, Ellen now has the habit of being overly concerned with how others are feeling or what they think of her, often to her detriment. She has a hard time setting boundaries or even knowing what her boundaries are. She is so used to catering to the needs of someone unpredictable and volatile that she never developed a relationship with her own needs and wants. It is taking her time to learn how to find her own center and break the habit of prioritizing other people's needs and opinions over her own. As a child, doing that would have put her in harm's way. The coping strategy that allowed her to have some control as a child is now causing her anxiety because she feels so out of control when in relationship with others.

Reclaiming our sense of center takes time. It requires us to attune to ourselves and find spaces and places where we can let go of our hypervigilance. For those of us who are in the habit of always attuning to others, it takes time to build this new habit. It can feel scary at first, because we're letting go of a coping strategy that got us through a difficult situation. Anytime we move from our survival self (who we had to be to survive) toward our authentic self (who we can become as we heal) it requires us to move through the fear we experienced in the past. I encourage you to take some time to reflect on where in your life your center is outside of yourself in a way that doesn't serve you. Track your body in different interactions and notice if there are some situations where you are able to be centered and others where you're not. Journal about it, write it down, and consider what centering practice might bring yourself and your needs into the moment. Start with easy stuff—for me, one of my first centering practices had to do with ordering takeout. In the past, when anyone asked what kind of food I wanted, my usual habit was to say, "I don't care," and defer to whatever the other person wanted. One day I decided to try something different and name my preference. It actually took some courage for me to say that I wanted Indian food, but I did it!

It's important to remember that being centered is not the same as being self-centered; it's about being centered in yourself. This actually allows us to be more present with others without needing to manage them. It can be a very generous act.

CENTERING PRACTICE

This is a standing practice that can also be done seated. Stand with your feet hip-distance apart, or find a comfortable seated position. Place one hand on your heart or the center of your chest and the other hand on your belly or solar plexus. Your eyes can be open or closed—whatever feels better. Feel the sensation of your hands on your body. Imagine a flame or a sphere at your belly—anything that can symbolize your center of power. Take a few deep breaths if that helps you settle.

Next, lean forward and come up on your toes, as if you were about to fall forward, then lean back onto your heels, then go side to side. Explore how your center keeps you from falling forward or back and can allow you, even if you do fall, to come back again. If seated, simply lean in each direction and feel for how your body keeps you from falling.

CENTERING PRACTICE WITH VISUALIZATION

Once you feel centered in yourself, imagine someone in your life standing near you. Notice if your capacity to stay in your center is harder in the presence of another person. (You can also choose to imagine someone who tends to take you off center). As you see them, put more of your attention on your hands on your body and your centering image. Feel in your body what it would be like to be centered while in relationship to someone else. (Hint: if this is really hard, you can shrink the person down in your imagination, or place them further away from you.)

Orienting to Present Time

The idea of being in present time is fairly straightforward. It's about being oriented to what is actually happening in the moment, not the future or the past. In the previous stories, we can see that both Rafael and Ellen were bringing their feelings from the past with them into new situations. They didn't do this on purpose, of course; the memories were imprinted in their bodies and minds. When Rafael heard the word "police," he was transported back to experiences of being unfairly harassed by police and had the impulse to defend himself. For Ellen, any relationship unconsciously reminds her of her father, and she thinks she needs to be hypervigilant to everyone else's feelings and needs in order to stay safe.

It can be complicated because sometimes our past experiences influence us to make choices in the present that put us in similar situations. For instance, Ellen may have a habit of forming relationships with people like her father who are actually unsafe because that's all she knows and that behavior is what she associates with love. We may also find ourselves in situations reminiscent of the past for reasons outside of our personal control. For example, Rafael may find himself unfairly treated by police again simply based on how he looks, not because he is drawn to the situation because it reminds him of his past. In these scenarios, both people are accurately assessing the situation and acting appropriately if they react as they did in their youth. But it doesn't have to be that way; part of healing can be finding a way to have a different reaction in a similar situation—a reaction that serves our best interests rather than undermining them.

When we are oriented in present time, we can make the distinction between when we need to be reacting to certain stimuli and when we don't. We are able to choose how to behave and maybe even make a different choice in situations that are similar to our past. Each time Ellen effectively sets a boundary with a person who is abusive, she disrupts her childhood pattern and experiences being empowered in the face of abuse. Being regulated is a state where we feel we can trust our assessment of our circumstances and we can respond appropriately.

Orienting practices can help us get our five senses present with what is actually happening rather than confusing what is present with a past event or circumstance. This can be a good one to do if you feel a panic attack coming on—simply look around the room and name the objects that you see, or colors. This can be settling because it brings you back to present time.

ORIENTING PRACTICE

From a comfortable position, begin to slowly look around the space you are in, taking in the colors and textures around you. Don't look for things you want to organize or tidy up, simply notice what is around you with curiosity rather than judgment. You can even name the objects you see. Slowly move your head when you do this, looking behind you and above. Also notice any smells, sounds, or textures with your hands. Notice if you spontaneously take a deep breath or settle when you do this. You can do this for up to one minute or even longer.

Breath

Just as it can be a tool for grounding, breathing deeply can always be a tool for self-regulation in general. When the breath is shallow, it triggers a sympathetic nervous system response, which is the stress response. When the breath is deep, it can trigger the opposite: the parasympathetic relaxation response. Sometimes simply taking a few deep breaths can help us settle and move out of overwhelm. Sometimes, however, trying to breathe deeply can make us feel more anxious because the breath feels stuck. If that's the case, don't force your breath. The grounding, centering, and orienting practices above can free up the breath so that it deepens automatically. Sometimes it can be more effective to do one of those practices first in order for the breathing practice to feel useful. In fact, when the breath deepens spontaneously, that can be a sign that you're settling and getting more self-regulated. Then breathing practices enhance that experience and help free up the diaphragm so that breathing deeply becomes easier overall.

BALLOON BREATHING PRACTICE

Imagine your lungs are like a balloon. When you inhale slowly, your ribs should expand in all four directions. Just like a balloon filling with air, your lungs expand when you inhale. On the exhale, feel your lungs contract. Don't force your breath; rather, think of allowing the breath to deepen. You can also find a rhythm where the inhales and the exhales are the same length. Do this for as long as it feels good.

COUNTING BREATH PRACTICE

Take a few moments to get grounded and settled. Start to slowly deepen your breath. Then start to find a rhythm where your inhales and exhales are about the same length. You can count up to six counts on the in-breath, then pause for a moment, and then count to the same number on the out-breath. Do this for two to five minutes.

SOUND PRACTICE

A great way to access the breath can be through sounding or singing. Simply humming, making a low toning sound or singing your favorite tune can open up your capacity to breathe deeply. Try it!

The Autonomic Nervous System

These tools for self-regulation impact the autonomic nervous system, which is what drives our stress response and our relaxation response. This branch of the nervous system is responsible for the involuntary processes of the body—things like heartbeat, digestion, blood flow, and breathing. It can activate us to take action when there is danger and calm us so we can settle when we are safe. Take a look at the diagram below for a map of the nervous system and its general functions.

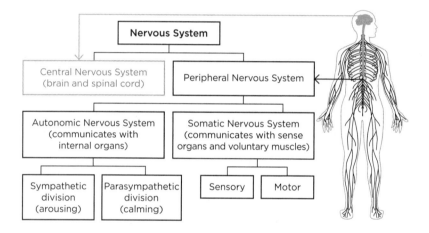

The autonomic nervous system sends signals to and communicates with our internal organs, including the blood vessels, stomach, intestines, liver, kidneys, bladder, genitals, lungs, pupils, and heart, as well as the sweat, salivary, and digestive glands. There are two main divisions of the autonomic nervous system: sympathetic and parasympathetic. The sympathetic nervous system is activating. It prepares the body for intense physical activity. It's responsible for the fight, flight, or freeze response. The parasympathetic nervous system does the opposite. It relaxes the body and inhibits or slows its high-energy functions.

When we are self-regulated we can flow between sympathetic and parasympathetic activation smoothly. We are able to deal with stressful situations and then recover once they are over. Imagine you have a conflict with a coworker, or someone cuts you off on the highway. Both experiences can trigger a sympathetic nervous system response where you get a surge of adrenalin—your heart rate rises, you get hot, and you feel a rush of energy mobilizing you to help you deal with a stressor. When the incident passes (the conflict gets resolved or you swerve out of the way and avoid a collision), you should be able to settle down (parasympathetic response), and feel relaxed again. (Look at the Regulated Nervous System figure.) When we're dysregulated it's much harder to settle after a stressful event. We might get stuck on high alert, even if we avert the car accident. We might get anxious and start playing out every possible scenario of a serious car accident for hours or days afterward. Or, after the conflict, we might find ourselves making generalizations about all people being mean, unscrupulous, or incompetent.

A Regulated Nervous System

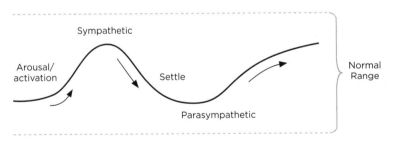

Another important response to stress, in contrast with fight, flight, or freeze, is the "tend-and-befriend" response.[3] This is a reaction designed to protect one's offspring and other vulnerable members of a group (tend) and seek out social groups for protection (befriend). When the tend-and-befriend response is activated, we seek out connection as a response to stress. This has important implications on how to cultivate healthy ways of dealing with stress. Feeling connected to others is an important key to managing anxiety. I'll be saying a lot more about that in chapter 6.

Stress and Trauma

Stress is not inherently bad. In fact, we need stress to motivate us. Dealing with stress is a necessary part of life, and facing difficulty can also give us grit and a sense of competency and personal agency. Trauma is a form of extreme, unmanageable, and terrorizing stress. Traumatic events are events that overwhelm our capacity to cope and respond, leaving us feeling helpless, hopeless, and out of control. Events themselves are not inherently traumatic; it is our response that determines if the event was traumatic. For now, let's think of stress and traumatic stress on a continuum, differentiated only by intensity. Both are characterized by a sense of overwhelm. Being overwhelmed by traffic or your workload is different from being overwhelmed because of the violent death of a loved one or having experienced a natural disaster, but on a physiological level there are some similarities.

Experiencing traumatic events doesn't necessarily sentence one to a life of pain and suffering as a result; in fact, traumatic events can lead to "post-traumatic growth"—one of my favorite terms. This refers to the idea that we can grow and even benefit from having to deal with adversity. Just like the butterfly whose wings get stronger by struggling to break free of the chrysalis, our struggles can give us the strength to soar to new heights.

Kelly McGonigal, a researcher at Stanford University, studies the impact of stress on humans. After years of telling people how detrimental stress was and how it was to be avoided at all costs, she dug deeper into the research and found out that she might be wrong. She found that stress wasn't necessarily as bad for us as we think. Neither was trauma. In one study, participants were asked about how many traumatic events they had experienced in their lives, as well as how anxious or depressed they felt. The results were a U curve. As expected, on one end of the curve, people who had experienced an extreme number of traumatic events were highly anxious or depressed.[4] But what surprised McGonigal was that on the other end of the curve, people who had experienced very little trauma were also highly anxious and depressed. Those in the middle, who had experienced a moderate number of traumatic events, were not. This points to the idea that overcoming adversity can make us strong and even happier, as long as we're not continually overwhelmed. It also helps us feel less afraid of future challenges because we know we can get through hardship.[5]

Happy people aren't people who have avoided suffering, they are people who aren't afraid of it. In his book *The Trauma of Everyday Life*, Mark Epstein, a psychiatrist and Buddhist practitioner, talks about "pre-traumatic stress disorder," which is the stress we feel when we worry about and anticipate bad things happening.[6] Trying to avoid suffering can be just as anxiety provoking as having had too much of it. This is why coming to peace with our anxiety and suffering is important.

How Animals Deal with Stress

Our nervous system is designed to deal with—and recover from—high levels of stress or trauma. We often hear stories about people overcoming incredibly difficult situations and thriving on the other side of them. Some of the most amazing people I know have survived the unimaginable. At the same time, we know that depression and anxiety are on the rise, especially in young people. So many of us are struggling to keep our heads above water, and whether we are dealing with unresolved trauma or chronically stressful circumstances, many of us are seeking tools to help us cope and feel better. It turns out there's a lot we can learn from how animals respond to overwhelming events.

Peter Levine, creator of the trauma healing modality Somatic Experiencing, found that animals in the wild don't seem to exhibit traumatic symptoms even though they are constantly threatened by predators. In his research, he observed animals in order to see what might be protecting them from the negative impacts of traumatic events such as inescapable attacks. His hope was that this could give us humans some insight into how we might deal with stress and trauma. The findings were fascinating. Basically, Levine found that animals have a way of discharging the energy mobilized for a fight-or-flight response. This allows them to return to homeostasis after a sympathetic stress response. Even after a near-death experience, they are able to go back to normal without carrying the experience with them.[7]

In a training I took with Levine, we watched a video of a possum being chased by a fox. Since the possum is too small to fight back or run away, it "plays dead," which is a sympathetic nervous system response also known as the freeze response. A freeze response is like having the accelerator and the brakes pushed at the same time. You're flooded with adrenalin and cortisol, tons of energy is mobilized to either fight or flee from the situation, your heart rate rises, digestion shuts down, and your breathing is shallow. Freeze is an adaptive response in nature; the fox is not a scavenger, so it's not interested in what it thinks is a dead possum. It sniffs around the possum a bit and then walks away in search of more viable prey. When the fox leaves, the possum starts to shake and tremble. Then it takes a deep breath and gets up and goes on with its day. It's not skittish or hypervigilant, expecting another fox around every corner. It doesn't go to the bar and get drunk to drown its feelings. It doesn't go pick a fight with its partner at home. The possum is fine. Unscathed. Why? Well, when you slow down the video, you can see that the possum is actually mimicking running. It is completing the flight impulse that it was never able to express. It is discharging the energy that was mobilized in order to fight or flee. So, when that possum gets up, it's thinking to itself, "I don't have to be afraid of foxes because I can get away from foxes!" Well, the possum probably isn't actually thinking, but it's *feeling* like it doesn't have to fear foxes because it has the capacity to deal with foxes if necessary.

Levine's research bore out the fact that this same principle applies to humans. In order to return the mind and body back to homeostasis after a traumatic event, we have to discharge the energy that was mobilized for the event. If we don't do that, the energy stays in our nervous system and can keep us trapped in this unresolved event—trapped in the past.

Stuck in the Past

There's a saying: "if it's hysterical, it's historical." This means that when we have an amplified response to an event, it's likely something from our past is coming up. If we don't discharge the stress energy, the unexpressed impulses want to find a way to be released and expressed, meaning they can get triggered without much provocation. Here's how it works.

Imagine that suddenly a bear appears at your door and enters the room. The moment you see the bear and feel threatened, the amygdala, an area of the brain that contributes to emotional processing, sends a distress signal to the hypothalamus. This area of the brain functions like a command center, communicating with the rest of the body through the nervous system so that you have the energy to fight or flee. During this sympathetic nervous system response, your brain secretes adrenalin and noradrenaline, which raises your heart rate and causes a rush of energy to go to your muscles. Your heart rate rises, your breath gets shallow, digestion shuts down, and energy rushes to your extremities, preparing you to run away or stand your ground and fight. Most of us cannot fight off a huge bear, so ideally you find an exit and run away to safety. Once you know you're safe, the parasympathetic "rest and digest" response kicks in. Your heart rate goes back to normal, digestion and diaphragmatic breathing resume, and your brain secretes dopamine and serotonin, which make you feel good. Unless you have a history of attacks by bears or other large hairy creatures, you would not be traumatized or seriously negatively impacted by this event. Remember, a traumatic event overwhelms our capacity to cope and respond. By running away, you coped and responded.

What if there was no other exit and you're not adept enough at martial arts to fight off a bear? Your third option is the freeze response. Remember, this is like having the accelerator and the brakes pushed at the same time. You've got all this energy mobilized to fight or run, but you're immobilized instead. As we saw with the possum, freeze is a natural response to an inescapable situation. If we discharge the energy mobilized during a freeze response, we won't necessarily be traumatized by the event. It's when we don't do this that we get into trouble. Imagine that the bear leaves, and you get word that it has been captured. You're safe! What do you do now? Ideally you shake and tremble like the possum, let yourself have a good cry, and then rest until you feel ready to move about your day. Unfortunately, many of us don't know that this is a good way to respond after such an experience. Instead, some of us might get up and try to get on with the rest of our day, not feeling justified in having an emotional response or physical release. Others might feel very emotional and overwhelmed and look for ways to soothe themselves or numb out to try and forget what just happened—to put it behind them.

Eventually, if you haven't successfully discharged the energy from the event like the possum, you may find that seeing a bear in a movie puts you in a panic, or seeing a big hairy guy walking down the street suddenly makes you feel like running. Even though there's no danger, these situations make you feel like you did when you saw the bear. Here is where we see the negative impact of undischarged traumatic stress: you're reading neutral cues as unsafe. The impulse to run from the bear gets triggered with stimuli that are reminiscent of the event. Even a loud sound can trigger this impulse now. It's like having a faulty alarm system at your house that goes off randomly or at the slightest provocation. It is no longer an accurate gauge of danger. Your GPS is off.

Wild animals are literally able to shake off trauma. They complete the fight-or-flight impulse that was thwarted. Humans tend to hold on to stuff or deny and minimize what we are feeling. This may serve us in the moment, but it can have a deleterious effect on our physical, mental, and emotional health.

Why Don't We Do What Animals Do? (Or Do We?)

Why don't humans just shake off stressful events like wild animals do? Why do we let stress energy build up to the point where it impacts our health and well-being? Why are we more susceptible to the deleterious effects of stress and trauma than wild animals?

Several factors come into play here. If the danger is always lurking, we may not ever have the space to shake it off and come to balance. If we are living in a chronically unsafe situation or if daily life involves other constant threats, we may not have the opportunity to decompress in this way due to having to remain hypervigilant and on high alert all the time. And if we are stuck in a fight, flight, or freeze state, we may not even be able to notice when we are safe and can release this pent-up energy. Others of us lead such stressful lives filled with constant stimulation that we don't have the chance to release our stress. For some, the "danger" is overwhelm at work, financial struggles, or isolation. Many of our modern stressors have to do with our lifestyles and become so normalized that we don't even realize things could be different and we could be feeling better.

It actually is our nature to discharge stress from our nervous systems when time and space allow. You may know this from experience. Have you ever had a traumatic or overwhelming experience and afterward your body starts to shake? That's your nervous system trying to release the stress energy. In fact, people shake so much after traumatic events that EMTs and medical personnel are often told to strap people down after car accidents or surgeries because they can reinjure themselves with the shaking. We're not different from animals (we are animals!), but we like to believe that we are. This may be part of the problem.

The Triune Brain

One thing that distinguishes human animals from other primates is the size of our neocortex. It makes up three-fifths of our brain. The brain is an incredibly complex organ, and scientists are discovering more and more about it all the time. One simple way to think about the brain is through the lens of the "triune brain" model that was formulated by physician and neuroscientist Paul MacLean. In this model the brain is divided into three parts: the neocortex or *higher brain*, the limbic system or *midbrain*, and the reptilian brain or *lower brain*. The higher brain is responsible for things like voluntary movements, communication, breathing, future planning, and thinking. We can think of it as *rational*. The midbrain is the "seat of our emotions" and affective memories— memories connected to intense emotions. We can think of this brain region as *emotional*. The lower brain is responsible for our involuntary processes such as heart rate, digestion, breathing (yes, breathing is a function of both the higher brain and the lower brain, which is why it's so powerful), sex drive, and the fight-or-flight response. We can think of this part of the brain as *impulsive* or *instinctual*.[8]

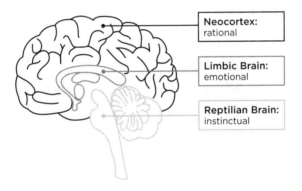

When we are in a dangerous situation, the midbrain and higher brain centers have to get out of the way, so to speak. We rely on the lower brain to get us out of danger even if we haven't wrapped our minds (i.e., our neocortex) around what is going on. If you've ever touched a hot flame, you'll notice that you automatically move your hand away from the flame before you even register what is happening. When you find yourself face-to-face with a bear, you're not thinking rationally (Where did this bear come from? What kind of bear is this?) and you're not connected to your feelings (I'm so scared right now; what if I get hurt?!). When our lives are under threat, the lower brain centers responsible for fight-or-flight take over. We are purely moving on impulse. To think or feel would slow us down and could jeopardize our safety.

When the possum is shaking off the trauma from the fox attack, it's not feeling self-conscious or wondering if others are going to judge it for shaking. It doesn't have a powerful enough neocortex to get in the way of its natural healing impulse. Humans, on the other hand, can override this impulse, thus trapping the energy in our bodies. When we haven't discharged the energy associated with a traumatic event, we can go into an impulsive state unnecessarily in situations that don't warrant it. If our fear gets triggered, we overreact and respond to an event in the moment as if it were a past traumatic event.

The ultimate goal is to have all three parts of our brain integrated and communicating with each other effectively. We need to be aware of our impulses and emotions so that we can regulate them and then act rationally. If we deny our impulses they can come out sideways, and if we suppress them they build up and get stronger. Most of us weren't taught how to identify and work with our emotions. Many of us have developed elaborate ways to avoid uncomfortable emotions and impulses at any cost. This is partly a result of our upbringing and culture.

We're Too In Control

Mainstream Western culture values the rational over the emotional or impulsive; it sees being stoic and "in control" as a sign of virtue and strength and being "wild" or "emotional" as a sign of weakness. Those of us raised in cultures like this are often taught to avoid being overly emotive and to deny or suppress the emotional and impulsive parts of us. We are taught to control ourselves from a very young age in our schools, places of worship, and homes. We are told to sit still, not be too energetic or "wild," and to "act civilized." I'm not saying we should act solely from our emotions and impulses; that would be chaos! We do ultimately want to speak and act rationally, but we also need to acknowledge our emotions and impulses. When we disconnect from the nonrational parts of ourselves, we cut ourselves off from our somatic wisdom. (*Soma* is another word for body.) Our need to be in control can get in the way of our natural impulses to express and release stress and trauma.

For instance, if you get into a car accident but don't get physically hurt, you might feel silly or "weak" if you start to shake or cry afterward. Even after the death of loved ones we often feel pressure to be "fine" quickly and not dwell in our sadness. Our culture tells us to "suck it up" and "grin and bear it" after stressful events. If we haven't sustained visible wounds, we don't often tend to the invisible wounds inside of us. We don't appreciate that our nervous system is loaded up with energy that needs to be released even if we didn't get hurt in any obvious way.

Humans need to reconnect to this instinctual capacity to heal. It's our nature to unwind from traumatic events. I've witnessed this firsthand. A student at a weekend workshop I was teaching once experienced a traumatic event when her car got a flat tire on a busy road during one of our lunch breaks. She stood by the AAA worker who was changing it, concerned that he'd get hit by one of the cars flying by. One car drove very close and knocked her over. She couldn't remember if the car actually touched her or if she just fell over, but it was a very scary experience for her.

When she walked back into the workshop for the afternoon session, she was clearly shaken up. Since she had already learned about the importance of discharge, she knew what she needed to do. We went back to her dorm room, and with me there to support her, she sat down and checked in with her sensations. She started to shake and tremble. It happened on its own; this wasn't something she was doing on purpose. I asked her if it was okay for her to be with the trembling and she responded, "Yes." Then her right arm started making a motion as if to brace from a fall, and her left arm started doing a pushing movement. She looked at me at one point and said, "This is so cool!" Her body was going through all the movements it never had the chance to actually make. It was completing the impulses to catch her fall and stop the car.

She then had the body memory of the car swiping her. She felt it touch her back. After about ten minutes, the trembling subsided and she felt tired. She lay down and slept deeply for an hour. Later, she walked back into the workshop smiling, grounded, and feeling good. She had discharged the energy that got mobilized when the car sideswiped her. At the time of the event, things happened too fast for her to brace for the fall or move away from the oncoming car. Those impulses were thwarted and that energy was stuck in her nervous system. When she released the energy afterward, she was able to return back to homeostasis and balance. The experience was now in the past.

People who don't understand how the nervous system works would likely deal with such a situation differently. They probably wouldn't know to take the time and space to shake, tremble, and release. They might feel that they should be okay because they didn't get injured. They might try different things to feel better—perhaps exercise and a hot bath, or alcohol or drugs—but without understanding that they need to fully discharge the energy, their efforts to merely manage the energy wouldn't yield the release their systems need. Managing our stress can mean using strategies that numb us out or make us feel better temporarily but do not shift our overall baseline sense of well-being. Managing our stress is exhausting. The other thing that happens is that this unreleased, pent-up energy lives on in our nervous system, so we never actually feel like we got away from the situation. We get stuck in the past or, rather, the past gets stuck in us.

In order to fully discharge the energy associated with a traumatic event, we need to have the space to feel safe enough to feel the intense impulses and emotions associated with the event and, like my student, allow the body to unwind and release. Sometimes we will literally shake and tremble but, especially if the event didn't just occur, sometimes the release can feel more subtle—like a tingling or settling or even an emotional expression like crying.

ENERGY DISCHARGE PRACTICE

The next time you experience a stressful event—anything from a tense interaction with another person to an emotional reaction to hearing or reading something to a physical trip or fall—before you move on to the next thing, pause. Notice your sensations and if you feel any impulses (to say or do something, or just to move in a particular way). Allow yourself to imagine doing that. You might make a sound or shake your body. You might simply be still and allow the pent-up energy to leave your body. Do this for a few minutes and then pause again and notice if you feel better or if anything has released. If you feel overwhelmed at all, use the tools of grounding, centering, or breath to support you.

*Please note: the work of discharging from serious traumatic events should be done with the support of someone with knowledge of trauma and how to release it. For a list of Somatic Experiencing practitioners in your area, go to www.traumahealing.com.

REFLECTION

What are some of your coping mechanisms that feel good in the moment but ultimately are detrimental or don't have a long-term benefit? Be honest. What are some coping strategies that you know work for you that may not be healthy and don't have any negative side effects?

ON and OFF People

Many of the examples I've shared describe states of high activation as a result of undischarged stress energy. These are what we call ON people in the Somatic Experiencing framework; we get amplified when we are stressed or triggered. I'm an ON person. When I'm stressed you'll find me furiously cleaning my house, creating elaborate spreadsheets to work out my budget for the year, or unnecessarily micromanaging my family. My stress makes me feel anxious and like I need to *do* something in order to feel in control. Sometimes this is good, and I can get things done efficiently and then feel better, but sometimes this behavior just stokes the fires of my anxiety and makes it worse. ON people can look anxious, hypervigilant, aggressive, or jumpy when we are out of balance. On a more extreme level we may be prone to panic attacks or serious health issues.

Other people do the opposite. We call you the OFF people. Unlike us ON people, you get tired, spacey, sleepy, or depressed when you are stressed or triggered. You shut down, withdraw, or disconnect when you're stressed. On a more extreme level you may find that you dissociate from reality or experience depersonalization or a sense of deadness inside.

Our ON or OFF reactions are similar to how electrical wiring in a building responds to a surge in voltage. If there's a sudden surge, either there's an explosion and appliances burn out or the surge protectors turn the electricity off to prevent that. Both situations—an explosion or the electricity turning off—are a result of too much energy moving through the wires. Our nervous systems are similar. When we have too much energy moving through us, we become dysregulated. We need to discharge the excess energy that we are holding so that we can be self-regulated.

As an ON person, I didn't know about OFF people until I learned about the different ways people respond to stress and trauma. I just assumed OFF people were lazy or spaced-out for no good reason. My husband is an OFF person. When he's stressed, you'll likely find him eating cookies and watching a movie, or asleep on the couch. He tends to slow down and shut down when he feels overwhelmed. It's helpful for me to know about OFF people because it allows me to understand that my dear husband is not lazy, he's just dealing with stress in his own way. And he can, on a good day, understand that I don't mean to be demanding and micromanaging when I'm stressed or anxious. I'm just trying to feel in control of my overwhelm. Sometimes our coping styles clash, but knowing that we are each, in our own way, trying to feel better can allow us to be patient with each other.

Some people can fluctuate in between ON and OFF.

A Dysregulated Nervous System[9]

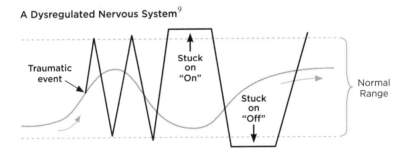

On Anxiety, panic, hyperactivity, exaggerated startle, inability to relax, restlessness, hypervigilance, poor digestion, emotional flooding, chronic pain, sleeplessness, hostility, rage

Off Depression, flat affect lethargy, exhaustion, chronic fatigue, disorientation, disconnection, dissociation, complex syndromes, pain, low blood pressure, poor digestion

REFLECTION

Are you an ON or OFF person, or both? What feelings, impulses, or behaviors do you tend to have when you are dysregulated?

Finding balance requires us to release the pent-up energy that is stuck inside of us. Although the concept is simple, actually doing it requires us to challenge the barriers that keep us from healing. These barriers include shame, cultural and familial norms that prevent us from acknowledging our feelings, and sometimes our very powerful rational mind. It requires us to regain and reclaim trust in our own body.

2

Trusting Your Body Again

Overcoming Obstacles to Feeling Good

KNOWLEDGE IS POWER. Understanding how something works, whether it's our own nervous system or a car's engine, can be a way to not get overwhelmed when things go wrong. Understanding the workings of the autonomic nervous system has been such a great tool for me and so many of my students and clients over the years. For those of us who live with anxiety, it can help reduce the shame we may experience for feeling the way we do when we understand that anyone can have an automatic response to stress that doesn't seem rational or reasonable.

I had the chance to offer some of this information to a small group of incarcerated men on a maximum-security ward who were taking a university class on healing. In our short time together, we talked about how stress and trauma can impact us, and I taught a few grounding and breathing techniques to help manage stress. I knew there was a lot of trauma in the room; not just the trauma that they experienced prior to their incarceration but also the stress of being incarcerated and often treated like subhuman criminals. A few spoke about their own fears and struggles quite openly. It was a stark contrast to the hard exterior that they had to construct to cope with prison life. Behind the muscles, tattoos, and blank stares was profound vulnerability.

One student, Joe, talked about his father taking him to the woods when he was six and forcing him to shoot animals. If he didn't comply, his father would beat him. Little Joe was hit and humiliated anytime he didn't comply with his father's demands. Joe had never thought that the abuse he'd endured as a child was connected to his drug addiction and violent behavior later in life. He didn't realize that the shaking and terror he felt every night when he want to bed or the terrible nightmares he had were signs of unresolved trauma. He used drugs to get away from the terrorizing feelings. His uncontrollable anger was rooted in all the ways he couldn't fight back as a child. He'd always thought that something was wrong with him, and he carried a lot of shame about it. With the information he got in this class, he began understanding that his behaviors were a symptom of trauma and his nervous system trying to regulate itself.

A few months after the class, I received a note from Joe. He shared that after twenty-five years with a diagnosis of post-traumatic stress disorder, or PTSD, and its unbearable symptoms, he was now starting to understand the very real impact childhood trauma had had on him. He shared that he was finally able to get some relief from the nightmares and anxiety for the first time. He had started a daily practice of the breathing and grounding techniques I had taught, which was helping with his sleep and mood. After he realized that the severe abuse he had endured as a child was the root of much of his suffering and actions, he was able to feel empathy for that little boy and thus begin to find compassion for himself as an adult. Joe shared that for the first time in his life he felt like he could forgive himself for all the mistakes he'd made. He didn't see himself as broken anymore, just a work in progress.

Joe is not alone in this experience. Knowing the workings of the stress response and our nervous system can give us some perspective so we can navigate what we are feeling. Often when we have just a sliver of awareness about what is going on inside of us, we have the chance to find a pathway through it.

Shame

Shame can be our biggest internal barrier to healing. I see this in so many people, especially if they are trying therapy for the first time. Some are hesitant to open up and share what is truly going on inside. It can take clients months, sometimes years, to share their deepest secrets. Some people have buried these secrets so far that they don't even realize they are carrying them. Shame isolates us. It makes us feel like we are the only person on the planet who feels the way we feel or has experienced the things we've experienced. We put a lot of energy into suppressing or hiding these memories, feelings, or experiences. We end up building a prison for ourselves because the walls we construct to protect and hide us end up trapping us.

Over the years I've heard stories from hundreds of people from all walks of life, and I've learned that so many of us are carrying very similar secrets. I share this not to minimize the true challenges that people have in their lives but to make clear that we humans have very similar core issues and fears—*I'm not enough, it was my fault, I'm not lovable, I don't belong, I'm bad.* Many people are plagued by these limiting beliefs. These beliefs are like monsters that we've locked up in a closet. They get louder when we refuse to acknowledge them. Shame is like the padlock on the door, preventing us from integrating the parts of ourselves that we most fear. Living in a performance culture where we see glossy representations of other people's lives on social media doesn't help. There's a saying: "Don't compare your insides to other people's outsides." This can be a dangerous habit that fuels our shame and isolation.

Releasing shame requires us to acknowledge, name, and feel the things we're ashamed of. The poem "The Guest House," by the Persian poet Rumi, offers a reminder to allow in our difficult emotions and impulses. He says that these things may be guiding us and "clearing you out for a new delight."[1] Rumi is inviting us to welcome all of our uncomfortable feelings with the knowledge that when we let go of our resistance it can free us up for something new. He invites us to embrace our uncomfortable feelings as our teachers. Sometimes our anxiety is this teacher.

Blame

Blame can be the flip side of shame. Shame is when we lash in, internalizing a feeling of being bad. Blame is when we lash out and attribute how we feel to external forces, blaming other people or events for our feelings. Sometimes it can be easier to blame the outside world for how we feel so that we can avoid ourselves. But blame puts the power outside of us, and that can also fuel our anxiety.

A client of mine, Rick, had this tendency to blame. He was always complaining about everything—traffic, his coworkers, servers at restaurants, the weather. You name it, he hated it. He experienced the world as conspiring to irritate him. One day he decided to take a vacation to get away from all the stress. He picked what he thought would be the perfect setting: a remote and quiet beach resort. When he returned, I asked him how his trip was. "Terrible!" he replied. "Why?" I asked. His response was, "I was sitting on a beach doing nothing and I was still mad. Only this time I couldn't blame it on my job or LA traffic." Rick had to confront himself on that beautiful beach, and that was way more uncomfortable than blaming the world for his problems. Both strategies—lashing in and lashing out—keep us stuck in our anxiety and suffering because they don't address the root cause of it.

I have also experienced blaming others as a cover-up to avoid my own difficult emotions. Many years ago, as a newer yoga teacher, I decided to check out the class of a famous instructor who I had been hearing about for a long time—Seane Corn. When I arrived, the room was packed, and many of the students who knew each other were happily chatting before class started. When Seane arrived, she greeted some of the students she knew personally and welcomed all of us. She had blond curly hair that looked perfect and a very hip outfit, and she was carrying a big fancy handbag and a Starbucks cup. Immediately I didn't like her, but I decided to stay to see what all the hype was about.

The class was physically challenging, which I typically enjoyed. In those days I could perform a handstand and I was naturally flexible, so many of the poses came easily to me. I had what some called an "advanced" practice because I could do difficult postures. But Seane did something I had never experienced—she talked to us about trauma and the mind-body connection during class. She kept telling us to notice our sensations and stay in our bodies. At one point, she had us in a hip stretch while she spoke about how we carry emotions in our body. She held us in that pose for a long time and, to be honest, I have no idea what she was talking about because the voices in my head were too loud. I was so mad at her! "Seane Corn with her puffy hair and perfect outfit. She must be some superficial yoga star wanting us all to feel like shit during her class." During that hip opener I swore I would never take this woman's class again because she was a terrible teacher and, worse, a terrible human just interested in fame and glory. I left the class all smug and judgy. "I would never teach a class like that. There was so much wrong with her sequencing. She should have her certification revoked!"

A few months later, a good friend told me that I really needed to meet his yoga teacher friend. To my surprise, he brought Seane Corn to lunch. Without enough time to think of an excuse to leave, I found myself eating a vegan meal with her. Within five minutes, I realized that this woman was awesome. She was down to earth, kind, humble, and wicked smart. We hit it off instantly and became friends. Eventually I decided to go back to her class and, once again, she put us in the hip-opening pose that I'd hated so much. I felt the rage arise. But this time, I couldn't blame my emotions on Seane. Now that I knew her, I knew she wasn't the cause of all those things I'd felt in her class the first time. This time I had to feel the rage rather than blame her for it. It scared me, but as I stayed with the feelings, the rage turned to grief and I found myself sobbing. I didn't know what it was about, but I felt so much lighter after class.

As I reflected on the experience later, I realized that a lot was going on for me the first time I walked into Seane's class. I think she represented the cool girls in high school—a group I was never a part of. She was confident, and everyone liked her. She seemed so comfortable in her own skin and looked so perfect from the outside—this was such a contrast to how chaotic I felt inside, but I didn't want to admit it. By making her bad, I could avoid my own shame and anxiety around belonging. I realized that this was how my family dealt with being immigrants and the ways we were different from the people around us. My parents would often tell us that we Lebanese people are better than Americans. Whenever we would see people behaving in ways we found unacceptable, my mom would comment, "In Lebanon this would never happen." I see now that we masked our shame and fear with bravado. If we could make everyone else out to be wrong, we'd never have to feel the vulnerability of being different. I learned early on that if I judged others I wouldn't have to confront the parts of myself that I disliked or feared. Once I paused and noticed my impulse to blame, it allowed me to tune in to my deeper feelings of shame, and then I could identify and work with my limiting beliefs.

REFLECTION

Do you tend to lash in or lash out? What are some examples of this?

You Have to Feel It to Heal It

"You cannot transform that which you refuse to feel." "You gotta name it to tame it." "What you resist persists." There are so many sayings that remind us that healing starts with feeling and acknowledging what needs to be healed. If this were easy, everyone would do it. One reason so many of us defend against feeling the difficult stuff is because we don't think we can handle it. On a physical level, we defend against sensations or emotions that we worry will overwhelm us or are associated with terrorizing experiences. Our body can start to feel like our enemy because being truly in it can force us to confront the intolerable.

This might be the point in the book where you decide that it might be a good idea to go binge-watch your favorite TV show, inhale a pint of ice cream, tell your partner how irritating they are, or organize your entire closet. You might also decide, as I did with Seane, that maybe I'm an idiot and you should have never wasted your money on this silly book. As I am suggesting that you look at the ways you might be defending against feeling, a part of you may get scared. It's normal. Have compassion for yourself.

If you need a break, do so consciously. You don't have to power through this content alone either. Consider getting the support of a trusted friend or therapist. Remember that you can reach out for support any time! Maybe instead of inhaling the ice cream, eat it slowly and enjoy it. Maybe instead of five episodes, watch two, and try to be patient with your loved ones through this process!

AWARENESS PRACTICE

Take a moment to pause and notice how you are feeling right now. Name any sensations, emotions, or images that are coming to you. Do you notice any impulses in your body? Say or write down what you notice. Don't judge what you feel; try and stay curious. Notice if acknowledging what is going on allows you to settle just a little. Do this for one or two minutes. You can use the tools of grounding, centering, and breath as well.

Broadening Our Window of Tolerance

It takes a lot of energy to deny our emotions. Shame and blame are not sustainable strategies. On a physical level, when we're not able to release the energy that we're holding on to, it builds up and we start to feel chronically dysregulated and uneasy. When we are really dysregulated, a lot of our energy gets used up managing our discomfort and not much is left for anything else. We can find ourselves exhausted by the smallest task. As a result, we may start to avoid potentially triggering or unpredictable situations, and even the slightest stressor can push us into overwhelm. One way to think of this is that we have a small window of tolerance; we are at capacity and more susceptible to the negative impact of stress or disappointment. Also, when our tolerance level is low, we can experience our environment in an amplified way—noises are louder, people let us down more easily, and we get really thrown off when things don't go as planned. It's like a bucket that is filled to the brim with water; just one drop can make it spill over.

Martha, a client who came to see me for therapy, experienced her life become much smaller after a traumatic event. As a young girl she had been gregarious and talented, always performing for her family in her living room, choreographing entire shows for everyone's delight. She loved to dance and pursued dance and performance arts in college. She was outgoing and sociable and loved travel and adventure. During her sophomore year, she was raped at a fraternity party by a young man in her social circle. She never told anyone. She felt ashamed; because she had been drinking, she blamed herself. After the incident, she stopped feeling comfortable dancing and started isolating herself from her friends. She stopped going to parties and social events and ended up dropping out of school during her junior year. She immediately married someone who felt safe to her. Martha never traveled again and built a life that minimized her risk and exposure to any unknown variables. Her world, which used to be big and exciting, became very small. It was all she could manage.

Martha came to see me for therapy forty years after the incident, which she still thought about every day. It still lived in her. She described feeling like a volcano about to erupt, and anytime she felt the energy, she either completely disconnected from her body or got busy taking care of everyone else. I worked with her to move through her shame and start to reconnect with herself again. First, she had to stay with the intense emotions that she was used to running away from. With my support and reassurance, she was able to feel her shame and stay with it. I had to gently remind her that it was not her fault that she had been raped. She began to let go of blaming herself.

When Martha was able to safely let herself feel the emotions and sensations around the event, they became less intense and more tolerable. She started to feel less afraid of what she was feeling inside. This broadened her window of tolerance—there was more she could feel without getting overwhelmed. As a result, she began to relax and open up her world, little by little. It took a lot of work, but she managed to let down some of the walls she had constructed to protect herself. She reported feeling like she could be in her body more now that she wasn't afraid of what she might find if she connected to it. Her body was no longer an intolerable place that held her secrets; it could be her ally and friend. She decided to accept an invitation with her friends to take a trip, and she even signed up for a dance class! Martha slowly let her world grow.

When our window of tolerance is big, we are less thrown off when things don't go according to plan or when challenges arise. Our bucket has space in it, so extra drops don't make it spill over. We can tolerate the discomfort, so we don't feel the need to run away from situations that could be difficult. When we avoid the unknown we keep ourselves from potentially positive experiences as well. In avoiding the bad stuff, we avoid the good stuff too. From a nervous system perspective, too much undischarged stress means we are already maxed out and we can't really deal with any more input, even positive input. When we release this energy, we have more space in our nervous system for life and what it brings. We can accept both joy and pain as facts of life.

Releasing Our Grip on Suffering

We can regain trust in our body, mind, and heart. It's about integrating all the parts of ourselves into our being so that we are not denying or fighting ourselves. When we are overwhelmed, we brace against this transformation. We're just trying to keep our head above water, and anything other than pure survival can feel out of reach. Letting go can feel like death. And yet when we can soften, even just a little, it can open the door to healing and liberation. This exercise using cornstarch and water is a great metaphor. Try it!

SOFTENING INTO RESISTANCE EXERCISE

In a medium-size bowl, mix two cups of cornstarch with one cup of water. With your hands, explore the consistency of the mixture. You will find that if you bang on the cornstarch it hardens, but if you touch it softly, your fingers will melt it. Pick it up and explore the effect on it when you are rough and when you are gentle. Notice if there is any resonance in your body as you do this exercise. (For extra fun add a few drops of food coloring.)

This exercise is symbolic of so much. Healing requires us to release our fear of our pain and suffering. When we resist the discomfort, it can't be transformed, just like the cornstarch mixture. When we surrender to what we are feeling, we can move through the resistance, transform it, and get to the other side. In order for the animal to shake and release the stress from its body, it has to let go and surrender to the natural process its body is going through. Humans inadvertently hold on to our suffering when we resist the pull to feel it and release it—sometimes because letting go feels scary and unpredictable, and sometimes because we're attached to our suffering because we believe it protects us. In fact, we're more wired to orient toward signs of danger or bad stuff than the good stuff. It's part of our survival.

Neuroception: Why the Bad Stuff Sticks

We are wired to look out for danger. It's part of our lower brain's strategy for keeping us safe. If you're on a hike and you read a long, curved form on the path in front of you as a snake and jump out of the way, that's much better than assuming it's a stick and being wrong. Looking for danger can save your life. The term for this is *neuroception*—our tendency to scan our environment for cues of unsafety; our propensity to notice the bad stuff. This is great if you're in the woods with snakes, but it's kind of a bummer if your environment is basically safe. In his book *Buddha's Brain*, Rick Hanson says that the brain is like Velcro to negativity and Teflon to positivity.[2] The bad is "sticky." It stays with us. The good, not so much.

In relationships, for example, someone can do one thing that hurts or betrays us and it can take many, many good deeds for them to regain trust again, if ever. As another example, I've been flying on airplanes my whole life without incident, but one plane had minor mechanical issues that disrupted my sense of safety on airplanes for several years. It took about twenty good plane rides to balance out that one bad flight. One of the goals of self-regulation is to train ourselves to notice the good stuff. This isn't about denying the bad. It's about not letting the bad override the good unnecessarily. If there's a bear in the room, you *should* be running—this is not the time to try and notice the beautiful painting on the wall. But when there is no danger and we are on high alert, we can use our tools of grounding, centering, orienting, and breath to shift that and settle. We can train ourselves to recognize when we are safe and to allow our nervous systems to settle and appreciate the good around us.

ORIENTING TO COLOR PRACTICE

Try this practice in two parts. First, look around the room you are in and notice all the blue objects.

Next, close your eyes and try to name all the red objects in the room.

NOTICING THE GOOD PRACTICE

Do you have the habit of focusing on the negative? Notice your thoughts and whether they tend to be geared toward amplifying the unpleasant or difficult parts of your day or life. Try this for one week: during your day, try and seek out things that are positive or pleasant. It could be a beautiful color or smell, a kind face, the soothing feeling of drinking warm tea. Every night before bed, make a list of any positive things that happened that day—even if they seem insignificant. Notice if you feel better as a result.

Remember that we don't want to bypass or deny what is difficult or unpleasant. It's just that if we can also feel what is positive, it can be easier to be with what isn't.

As you may have learned from this practice, we find what we're looking for. It's hard to name the red stuff when you're just looking for blue. It's hard to notice the good when we're in high alert looking for signs of danger. One thing we can do is shift our focus. This is not about denying the unpleasant things, it's about deliberately noticing and even amplifying the things in our day or in our lives that are positive, pleasant, or reassuring. Sometimes shifting what we focus on in the external world can shift how we feel internally. The opposite can also be true, as you may have learned from the resourcing practices we've already practiced.

Bypassing Our Emotions

If I had experienced the bear scenario from chapter 1 twenty years ago, my response once I was safe would have been something like this: I would have instantly disconnected from my emotions and decided that the bear came for a reason. I might have concluded that I had actually manifested the bear myself in order to learn some major life lesson. I would have looked up the symbolic meaning of bears and written some provocative journal entry about "bear medicine" and why I needed it at that point in my life. Then I'd have gone home, eaten a large jar of Nutella chocolate spread, and fallen asleep. I would have then repeated the chocolate-eating behavior any time memories of the bear surfaced.

This kind of response is what is called *bypass* or *spiritual bypass*. It's a way to avoid actually feeling painful feelings by justifying them or prematurely making meaning of them. We definitely can learn from our challenges and make meaning out of them—in fact, this is an important part of healing—but we can't skip the step of engaging with the feelings associated with the experience. If we do, the "lesson" will probably be fruitless. I did this with a health challenge. In my twenties, I was diagnosed with cervical dysplasia, also known as "precancer." As soon as I got the diagnosis, I dove into research on healing on a physical and energetic/psychological level. I read up on the second chakra and found the symbolic meaning of this illness (wounds around relationships and sexuality), and I learned about holistic medicine protocols and did a bunch of fasts and cleansing programs. Eventually I had the cells removed and have been healthy ever since.

One thing I never did during the whole experience was cry or admit that I was scared. I immediately went to finding a solution. And as soon as I was healthy, I went right back to my old behavior of numbing out with sugar and denying my feelings. Oh—and I also went back into the dysfunctional relationship that I thought this illness represented! You see, I never integrated the symbolic insights emotionally or psychologically. Often when we face a major challenge, it can benefit us to go into action mode in order to address it. We don't want to get stuck in our emotions and miss an opportunity to address what is going on in a practical way. It's vital, however, to eventually allow ourselves to feel and process the emotions that may have been minimized or set aside in a moment of crisis. If we don't, they get stuck in us and we may not be able to truly move on or learn from the situation.

In my case, my decades of avoiding my feelings contributed to the anxiety crisis I described in the introduction to this book, where I was hit with anxiety and chronic fear about *everything*. I was scared of flying, I worried that my husband was going to get ill and die, I thought that my kids were doomed because I wasn't raising them right. I felt scared in cars unless I was driving, and often I would wake up with my heart racing even though there was nothing wrong. I even thought I might have heart problems because the sensations were so intense. I felt so fragile and vulnerable, like life could just take me down any moment. It took me almost three years to work through these fears, even though I had all the tools. I'd been teaching on these topics for decades, but I was still avoiding my most vulnerable feelings about my own mortality and the mortality of those I loved.

I had to face the fact that even becoming an expert in trauma was, on some deep level, an attempt to avoid having to face my own trauma. I feel comfortable supporting people who are struggling, but being the person struggling myself is something I have avoided most of my life. In order to heal my anxiety, I had to face it, full on, and feel it. I had to let it bring me to my knees. I used the tools that I'm sharing with you in this book. I had to sit with my biggest fears and wrap my mind, heart, and soul around the fact that life includes suffering and I am not exempt from the human experience. I had to challenge the defense mechanisms I had built since I was a child, and face the feelings I wasn't able to face then. It's hard work, and I needed the support of my therapist, teachers, family, and friends along the way.

REFLECTION

How did you cope with challenging emotions or situations as a child? Do you still have any of those habits? Which ones serve you and which ones don't?

What We Inherit from Our Family

I'm trying to teach my children about their emotions and impulses from a young age. In our family, we do our best to not shame big feelings so that we can teach our kids how to be connected to all the parts of themselves without shame. When my kids were six and three, my younger son, Marley, broke a Lego building that my older son, Sebastian, had made. The scene went something like this: Sebastian is trying to hit his little brother, and I'm standing between them. Sebastian says, "Marley messed up my Legos and I'm so mad! The only way I'm going to get the anger out of my body is if I punch Marley in the face!" There is already some success evident in this scenario. Why? Because he is naming his emotions and impulses without shame. I explain to him that he can't hurt his brother and we need to find another way to get the anger out of his body. We get Marley to safety and then Sebastian tries a few things. First, we try pushing our hands into each other and growling. Then he tries screaming into a pillow. Finally, he goes outside to jump on the trampoline in our yard and yells to me, "Mom! I'm on the trampoline! It's working!"

When you reflect on the messaging you got in your family, does it help you understand what you do with your emotions and impulses today? Most people who I ask this question of report that they were either told to suck it up or were shamed for their big emotions. Some people feel that only certain emotions were tolerated. Many of us were taught to distract or numb out from painful feelings; we reach for food, shopping, or entertainment instead of being with the discomfort. A very small number of people report feeling like they were taught to be compassionate toward themselves around their emotions and impulses. Most don't feel they received any tools to deal with overwhelming feelings. This is because our parents didn't have the tools themselves. If they did, they would have shared them with us. They did the best they could with the tools that were passed on to them.

REFLECTION

What were you taught to do, explicitly or implicitly, with your big impulses and feelings in your family of origin?

When my son Sebastian was about fourteen months old, he fell off a low stool. He was crying, so I came over to comfort him by sitting with him and holding him. I asked him, "Do you feel hurt or scared?" He responded, "Scared." I kept myself calm and just sat with him. Once he settled, I gave him a little space to see what he might want to do next. He chose to get back on the stool and jump off. He did this several times. From a biological perspective, I imagine he was wanting to redo the event until he mastered it so that his nervous system could feel like he jumped off that stool, rather than falling. Another time, he fell off a bed. This time he wanted me to hold his hand and jump off of it with him. Yet another time, he fell off a bed, but my mom was with him this time. I was in the next room. I heard him fall and cry. Then I heard my mom pick him up and say to him, "You're okay! Here, do you want a candy?" In her care for him (and possibly in her inability to tolerate his discomfort), she wanted to distract him from his feelings. Ultimately this can send the message that we are supposed to distract ourselves from our emotions. Distracting can indeed help in the moment, but as we see over and over, not acknowledging our strong feelings can contribute to our anxiety and dysregulation.

The more we are able to admit our impulses, no matter how terrible or inappropriate they seem, the less likely we are to act on them. One day when Sebastian succeeded in hitting his brother, he said to me, "Mom, my *body* told me to do it; you tell me to listen to my body!" His body told him to hit his brother because he was overwhelmed with emotions, as children often are, and in the moment, it was all he felt he could do.

My imperfect response to Sebastian's line about his body telling him to hit his brother was, "My body tells me to hit you sometimes, but I don't do it." At which point my younger son, Marley, said, without missing a beat, "Well, that's because you do yoga!" Even at such a young age, he knew that I did something to help me self-regulate and not act on my impulses. Part of why I could regulate my responses in these moments of anger is because I admitted to myself that I had the impulse to hit my child, and I used my practice of grounding and regulating myself to not act on that impulse. I also had a regular practice (yoga) of connecting with my breath and body, which strengthened my self-awareness and my capacity to regulate my emotions and behavior.

What We Inherit from Our Ancestors

Coping strategies get passed on to us from our parents. They get theirs from their parents, and so on. Most of us have histories of violence, genocide, slavery, and/or colonization in our ancestry. Some of our ancestors were the victims and some were the perpetrators. Both are traumatic in different ways. For people who were being persecuted, it usually wasn't safe to express emotion, and many impulses had to be repressed for the sake of survival. For people who went through the unimaginable, repressing their feelings may have been the only way to survive. For people who perpetrated atrocities, often there is massive shame, secrecy, and denial around their actions.

These survival strategies can get passed on from generation to generation. When we don't know the roots of these behaviors, we normalize them and think they are an inherent part of our culture. Unprocessed trauma that happens to groups can get coded as culture. Joy DeGruy, author of a book called *Post Traumatic Slave Syndrome*, talks about the habit of some contemporary African American parents to downplay how smart or talented their children are.[3] She connects this to slavery, when children who were particularly gifted or strong would get taken away from their parents to be sold or go work elsewhere. Back then, enslaved parents would hide their children's gifts in order to not lose them. In some families, that habit lives on today. Enslaved people also passed on incredible strength and perseverance to their offspring. Both the wounds and gifts of trauma get passed on, not just through cultural practices and rituals, but through our DNA.

Rachel Yehuda, a professor of psychiatry and neuroscience at Mount Sinai School of Medicine in New York, examined the neurobiology of PTSD in Holocaust survivors and their children.

She found that the children of survivors who had PTSD had low cortisol levels like their parents, predisposing them to relive the PTSD symptoms of the previous generation. She found similar patterns in the children of war veterans. Her research showed that trauma can be passed on in our genes—not just our culture. As Yehuda explains, from a biological standpoint the purpose of an epigenetic change, or a change in the functioning of our genes, is to expand the range of ways we and our future generations respond to stress.[4] Thus, those of us whose parents experienced trauma are born with a genetic predisposition to deal with trauma that can benefit us if we are facing similar challenges. Some of our ancestors had to be incredibly strong in order to survive, and that gets passed on to us too.

REFLECTION

Consider again how you were taught to deal with big emotions as a child. In what way might have these norms and rules been necessary for your ancestors? How might these have been survival strategies?

What gifts and strengths have you inherited from your family and ancestors? What traditions or beliefs are positive coping strategies and supports for you?

For people who are adopted and may not know their DNA ancestry, and for people whose ancestors were forcefully separated and uprooted, like enslaved Africans in the Americas, the work of understanding ancestral inheritance can be limited. Since we carry this inheritance in our body and mind, there is still an opportunity to get curious about what habits we hold that could be from previous generations. We might not know if the answers that come to us are literally true, but they can be meaningful nonetheless. Today some people are choosing to do DNA testing to understand their ancestry and explore this part of themselves. For some it can be helpful to have this information and learn more about the places and cultures that they come from; for others, this is not necessary and their process of exploration can be guided by their present experience and circumstances.

Resilience

People are incredibly resilient—superheroes, if you ask me. So many people and entire communities have survived and thrived despite generations of trauma and violence. Resilience is typically defined as the ability to bounce back from difficulty. It's a buzzword in the trauma and education literature, where research suggests that building resilience can help people recover from traumatic events. But sometimes the word seems to be used in unhelpful ways that can undermine the legitimate challenges and suffering that people endure.

I have a client who absolutely hates the word. She survived the 2013 Boston Marathon bombing. People she loved, who were there to watch her, were standing right by one of the bombs; they lost limbs and had their lives permanently changed by the event. When she hears the word "resilience," and the implication that she could "bounce back" from such a tragic event, she is enraged. Surviving a bombing is not something you bounce back from and return to normal from. There is no normal, ever again, after a bomb explodes in front of you. What there is, however, is trans-formation. Trauma and difficulty change us—sometimes for the better, sometimes for the worse; often, it's a mixed bag. My client's whole life changed after this incident. It will never be the same. She is now a trauma therapist herself. She holds space for people going through unimaginable things in a way that no one else can.

Does she still suffer as a result of that day? Absolutely. Has she been transformed by that event? Absolutely. I think that is true resilience.

I define resilience as our ability to be transformed by difficulty. Sometimes this means finding wholeness again and sometimes it means finding a new way to be whole. Sometimes it means, like the Japanese art of *kintsugi*, filling our cracks with gold. In this art form, cracks are not covered up or disguised but honored as part of the history of an object. We work to integrate by including and accepting all the parts of ourselves—our brokenness and our brilliance.

Resilience is not just about recovering from difficulty, it's also about having a sense that we can handle whatever difficulties might arise in our future. Bessel van der Kolk, a trauma researcher and author of the book *The Body Keeps the Score*, says that trauma is a "failure of imagination."[5] One loses the capacity to envision that things might turn out better than they have before. For someone living with anxiety, life can feel like a constant repetition of a terrorizing experience. We are all unconsciously living into an imagined future—whether we see it as better or worse than what we have already experienced. Regaining our capacity to reimagine our life and live into a future that feels hopeful and bright is part of resilience and transforming trauma.

Trusting the Body Again

It's not always easy to be with ourselves, especially our uncomfortable feelings. When we can't be with that stuff, many of our actions will be an attempt to run away and avoid it. Also, when we run away from the bad stuff, we run away from an important source of wisdom that we need in order to navigate our life—our body! Many of us are not given the tools to go inside and figure

out how to trust our bodies, minds, and hearts. We live in a culture that normalizes and encourages looking outside of ourselves
for satisfaction and well-being. We are bombarded with messages:
"If you feel bad, just buy these shoes, or lose some weight, or find
the perfect partner." We are taught early on to look outside of ourselves for happiness and satisfaction.

Regaining trust in ourselves can be a lifelong journey. We
are layered beings, and life will always bring us new challenges
and opportunities. Healing is more like a spiral than a straight
line. We will find ourselves revisiting issues that we thought we
had resolved, only to find that there is more work to do. Understanding the workings of our body, brain, and nervous system can
be a powerful resource for navigating the ebbs and flows of this
journey. Using the practices that we've learned so far to keep
ourselves grounded and to release and discharge stress can help
keep our minds clear and our hearts open so we can do the important work of growing, learning, and becoming more whole and
authentic.

3

Reclaiming Our Capacity to Heal

Tools for Releasing Stress and Anxiety

IT IS OUR nature to recover from difficulty. We are literally wired for this, just like animals in the wild. Many of us have been socialized to deny and suppress these instincts, and our bodies, minds, and hearts are confused and disoriented as a result. This chapter is filled with some key ideas and practices to support healing and integration in your body, mind, and heart. Healing also requires us to look at our relationships to other humans, nonhuman animals, and the planet itself. That is coming later. For now, we'll continue to focus on the nuts and bolts of regulating our nervous system.

Interoception

As discussed previously, with our natural tendency to notice the bad and a buildup of undischarged stress from our past, coupled with living in a culture that doesn't support us to feel and release stress, it makes sense that so many of us are anxious. We need to learn how to discharge the stress energy that has built up in us. It all starts with being able to feel what is going on for us without getting overwhelmed. For so many of us, that is the scariest part. But it doesn't have to be.

One key to self-regulating and feeling like we can cope with what is happening to us is *interoception*. Interoception is the perception of the state of the body, specifically our internal organs. Interoception has been correlated with the ability to make accurate decisions in social science research.[1] (*Exteroception*, on the other hand, is our ability to sense what is outside of us; it refers to our five senses: sight, hearing, smell, touch, and taste.) Interoception has to do with knowing when we need to use the bathroom and if we are hot, cold, or aroused. When you become aware that your stomach is tight and your heart is racing, that is interoception. When our fear or anxiety gets triggered, our interoception might tell us that something bad is happening. It's like having alarm bells go off inside of us. When we are stressed and triggered into a sympathetic nervous response in our bodies, even if what is happening in the outside world isn't harming us, we may interpret external cues with our interoception, not our exteroception. The outside world seems to validate how we already feel and we don't take in evidence to the contrary because it doesn't match our internal state. To put it simply, when we are scared or anxious, we tend to only see things around us that confirm our fear.

When my son Marley was a baby, I noticed that he had some red dots on his legs. After I put him to bed, I did something you should never do—I googled it. In ten minutes, I was convinced he had West Nile virus. We had just come home from a trip to the East Coast and he could have gotten bit by an infected mosquito. I got very anxious reading the symptoms of this virus, and, because my nervous system was in a sympathetic state of high arousal, I believed that he had these symptoms. Luckily, I knew that I had worked myself up and couldn't trust what I was feeling. So I called in my husband, who was totally calm, and asked him to look at the list of symptoms of West Nile virus. He gently reflected back to me that our son had *none* of these symptoms and was most definitely okay. He was right. My internal alarm bells were sounding, and I was reading cues out in the world through my anxious internal experience.

Many people are not in the habit of practicing interoception. We only feel our bodies when they are hurting or something very obvious or extreme is happening. As with our tendency to cling to negative thoughts, many of us also tend to only notice when we experience unpleasantness in our bodies. When we are in the habit of checking in with our sensations more regularly, we get better at distinguishing when we are triggered into fight, flight, or shutdown from when we are regulated and getting accurate information about the external world. I like to call this "getting fluent in the language of the body." When we are familiar with being connected to our sensations, we're better able to distinguish the ones that are signaling to us something real from the ones that are a reaction to our fear getting triggered.

I credit my interoceptive capacity in getting through my struggles with anxiety. For how difficult it was, I could always tell when my body was overreacting, and I rarely confused my anxiety for an accurate assessment of a situation when it wasn't. It was a difficult phase for sure, but even at its worst, I always had some perspective about what was really going on for me.

INTEROCEPTION PRACTICE

Take a moment to notice what you are feeling in your body right now. Not just the stuff that feels very obvious—for example, a hurt knee or a stomachache. Notice what other sensations you feel. You can start from the feet up. Try and notice temperature (hot, warm, cold, cool), texture (buzzing, tingling, smooth, rough), tension or space—you might even notice that there are parts of your body you don't feel. How does your belly feel? Your chest? Your hands? Your head? What is feeling good? What feels neutral or uncomfortable? Do you see colors or images as you sense into your body? Try to be curious rather than judging.

You can take this to the next level and draw a body map. Draw an outline of a body (don't worry, it doesn't have to be a great work of art) and fill it in with words or images and colors that describe how you feel in each area.

If this practice feels silly, good! It means you're doing something new. It's always awkward to try new stuff. I like to say that if it's not awkward, then you're not growing. Part of healing is disrupting the habits that don't serve us and cultivating new ones that do. The new ones will always feel funny at first. You may not be sure if you're doing it right. That's okay. Just getting in the habit of asking yourself, "What am I feeling in my body right now?" gets the process going. Don't just focus on your joints, muscles, and bones; notice your belly, your chest, your breath, and more subtle sensations. Sometimes you might notice emotions. In that case, ask yourself, "How does this emotion feel in my body?" You might be surprised at the new information that becomes available to you.

Fear or Intuition?

Sometimes it can be challenging to know if what you feel is accurate or not—if it's intuition or fear, for example. My definition of intuition is that it's the wisdom of the body, heart, and mind. It's when our sensations, feelings, and thoughts are consistent and coherent. One way to know that your fear might be being triggered is if your emotions and sensations are exaggerated; you might not be responding to what is in front of you but rather to a memory it triggers. For instance, if you find yourself flying into a rage when your partner is five minutes late or in a puddle of tears when you burn some toast, it could indicate that something else is going on beyond what just happened in the moment. Maybe there's a history with your partner that needs to be addressed or a well of emotion that is craving expression. Sometimes you might have an amplified response to something because you're already in a stressed-out state and the smallest thing is just too much. The more versed we become in knowing our own body and sensations, the better we get at making those distinctions for ourselves.

DAILY INTEROCEPTION PRACTICE

For the next few days, try and notice your sensations and emotions throughout your day. Track what you feel while interacting with certain people and doing certain activities. Look for subtle things, not just the big, obvious feelings. Also, try to avoid just looking for the uncomfortable stuff—notice when you feel grounded or good too. Notice your breath, what's happening in your shoulders and belly, and if you feel activated, shut down, or in balance. You don't need to change anything; just notice. The more you get in the habit of feeling your sensations with curiosity, the more you can refine your GPS and let it steer you right. Consider setting an hourly alarm on your phone to remind you to check in.

One day my boys were wrestling (as they do on most days) and Sebastian pulled a blanket from Marley's mouth, which resulted in a tooth getting yanked out. Marley was scared at first. His mouth was bleeding, and he'd never lost a tooth before. As I sat with him while he sucked on an ice cube, he remembered that, coincidentally, at school that day they had made small pouches for lost teeth. His tears dried up and he got excited about what treat the tooth fairy might bring him. He quickly got up and put the tooth in the pouch under his pillow. He was quite happy for the rest of the evening. When I was tucking him in at night, I asked him how he felt. "Great!" he exclaimed. Then I asked him how his body felt. "Worried," he replied. "Where do you feel the worry?" I asked. "In my belly," he responded, and started to get visibly upset again. Then I asked him how his legs felt. "Strong!" he exclaimed, and he began to settle. I asked him what color the worry was, and he responded that it was red. The strong part was white. I invited him to feel both what was strong and what was worried. I saw his body relax, and he looked up at me and asked, "What does white and red make?" "Pink," I replied. "It's all pink now," he said happily, and fell asleep. The next morning, before even looking under his pillow for what the tooth fairy brought, he came to my bed and exclaimed with delight, "It's magenta now, Mommy!"

On one level, Marley was genuinely excited about the tooth fairy, but he also found a good way to avoid the unpleasant emotions by focusing only on his excitement. When I invited him to really check in, he found that there was still some fear in his body. When he was able to be with the fear with my support and also notice that his legs felt good, his fear shifted almost immediately into a more bearable emotion. Checking in with our own bodies more regularly can help us better understand how we're feeling deep inside, even when we tell ourselves everything is fine. And checking in with what feels secure or safe in our bodies can also help us find a way to be with what feels uncomfortable or scary.

The Wisdom of the Body

The body can sometimes know something before the mind does. The HeartMath Institute has been conducting research on what it calls *coherence*, a state of balance and flow between the heart and the brain. Coherence implies a state of harmony, stability, and well-being. Coherence can be another word for self-regulation. In one research study, subjects were seated in front of two decks of cards. They were told that they would win one dollar for each card that was bigger than a seven. One deck was stacked with better cards, but they didn't know that. The researchers were measuring heart rate and sweat. They found that about three minutes into the study the subjects' heart rates went up and they started sweating when they were picking from the better deck. Their body signals were getting excited. It took seven minutes for them to realize which was the better deck and start picking from it more. In other words, their body knew which one was the better deck before they realized it cognitively. Other research has shown that subjects who are better at interoception do better overall on tasks like this than those who aren't.[2]

How often do you think that your body might be giving you information about your surroundings, but since you're not paying attention, you miss it? Many people don't notice enough and miss important cues. Some people tend to be hypersensitive to these cues. They notice too much in their body, and it can be distracting. Practicing interoception can help us develop this fluency of the body. It's a way to fine-tune your GPS so that it's more trustworthy. We can develop a connection to a stream of information that is always available to us to help us navigate the world around us and build resilience.

REFLECTION

What is your relationship with your body? Describe it as if your body were another person and you're describing the dynamic between the two of you.

We Have "Civilized" Ourselves Away from Our Natural Healing Impulses

As I mentioned in chapter 2, shame can be our biggest barrier to being integrated and whole. The more we touch into the uninvestigated parts of ourselves, the more we may tap into stuff we find embarrassing or not in alignment with who we want to be. We all have parts of ourselves that we wish didn't exist. Social norms tend to dictate what types of behaviors and feelings are "acceptable" and which ones aren't. Being rational and in control is highly valued in most Western cultures, while being emotional is not. This conditioning starts in our families and is especially hammered into us at school and in professional settings where compliance can help create order and cooperation. In most school settings, children are expected to sit still for hours and to pay attention to teachers without wiggling, squirming, or making noise. We are taught to suppress our natural urge to move and explore from an early age. We are taught to be compliant and "civilized," not "wild" or out of control.

Tyrone was suspended in the ninth grade for punching a hole through a wall when he was angry. He was also kicked out of the honors music class he had qualified for because of the incident. He started using drugs to numb his rage, and he slowly withdrew from a world that felt harsh and intolerable. Years later, still struggling with mental health and addiction issues, he reflected to me that his school had punished him for his inability to manage his emotions, but no one ever taught him how to manage them. On top of that, his school had taken away the one resource—music—that had been a way for him to express himself and begin to work through his rage. He had internalized the idea that he was bad and only later on in life did he realize that what he deserved was support and tools to manage his emotions, not punishment and being ostracized for not knowing how.

Although it's important to create and abide by some group norms in order to reduce chaos, this can be taken too far, as we can see in Tyrone's story. When we are forced to disconnect from the spontaneous and wild parts of ourselves, we get cut off from impulses that support us in healing and releasing stress and trauma. As research professor and author Brené Brown says, "Numb the dark and you numb the light."[3] If we're not given adequate space to express ourselves appropriately, we can take on this need for compliance, to the detriment of our own self-regulation and authenticity. We internalize the voice that tells us, "boys don't cry," "you're overreacting," "you're too much," and so forth. We can become ashamed of the parts of ourselves that need to be felt and expressed the most, so we deny and suppress them. This is the root of much addiction—we use substances (or shopping, food, or even work) to distract us from our deepest feelings and impulses because we are ashamed of them or they feel out of control. We all have these raw, animalistic emotions and impulses. It's that primitive part of our brain that wants us to fight off threats, procreate, and protect. (These impulses are also creative, expressive, sexual, and pleasurable.) But we have "civilized" ourselves away from our natural healing impulses and creative expression.

When we are able to normalize the fact that all of us have emotions and impulses that we may not be proud of or that are unpleasant or "wild," we can then work to channel these impulses appropriately. Remember, some of these impulses are residual, unexpressed impulses from traumatic events. They will show up in "inappropriate" situations because they want to be expressed and released. Some people build their entire life around hiding the parts of themselves they most fear exposing. Marco's story is not unique.

Marco was one of the top cardiac surgeons in the country.

When he came to see me, his main complaint was severe depression and painfully low self-esteem. This was surprising given that he was such a well-respected physician. He shared with me that he had been molested as a child. He was so ashamed of it that he became an overachiever, always trying to prove that he was worthy of respect and love. He also was addicted to porn, which he felt very ashamed of. He had never had a healthy sexual relationship and he spent his whole life focusing on work. He had never gone to therapy before because he was too embarrassed to share any of this, but when he came to see me he had decided he was ready to face his challenging feelings. Through our work together, Marco was able to finally admit some of the complicated feelings that can arise with molestation, feelings that haunted him years later—the pain and fear from the abuse but also some enjoyment because he got special attention from someone he looked up to, even though the attention was inappropriate and harmful. As he was able to work through these feelings, he was able to heal his porn addiction and stop watching inappropriate content that replicated his childhood trauma. He began to open up to having healthy intimacy with another consenting adult. As he was able to have compassion for the little boy who was abused, he could start to believe that he was worthy of love and safety, and that he didn't have to always be saving lives in order to be loved. He could be loved for who he is, not just all that he does.

What Is "Normal" Anyway?

Some people are burdened by shame and anxiety because they have been told—explicitly or subliminally—that who they are is not okay. These messages can come from society, family, school, religion, and more. When we internalize this judgment, it is toxic and harmful. In general, Western social norms tend to value and encourage people to be "put together," productive, not too emotional or "wild." There are also cultural norms around gender, age, body size, sexuality, race, ability, class, and more. If you don't fall into what is considered "normal," acceptable, or most valued in your culture, you might be shamed or even hurt for who you are. People whose very existence is marginalized or pathologized by society are at risk of having anxiety—when the core of who you are is seen as broken or less valuable it's very hard to feel secure in the world.

The idea of normality is a social construct—not a tangible fact—and it varies greatly generationally and culturally. In his book *Normal Sucks*, Jonathan Mooney explores how people in power have used the concept of "normal" for centuries to maintain their own power and to dismiss and devalue the people and perspectives they consider to be "other."[4] Who and what is considered normal, historically, has reinforced the status quo. For instance, in the 1930s, the first longitudinal study of "the normal person" was conducted to determine what characteristics made someone "normal." This study was conducted at Harvard Medical School and was inherently biased because it studied educated white men and then generalized the results to all of humanity. Most psychological standards of normal behavior and affect are based on biased research. Even though things are evolving and the biases inherent in much social science research are being challenged, many of us have internalized standards of what's "normal" that may not serve us and are based on flawed assumptions.

REFLECTION

In the culture you grew up in, what qualities were valued and devalued? Are there aspects of your personality and identity that were valued or devalued? How did you respond to this?

Western culture also values independence and qualities that support the myth of "rugged individualism," a belief that if you work hard you can succeed on your own. Individualistic cultures value qualities like independence, assertiveness, and self-reliance, in contrast with collectivist cultures where characteristics like being self-sacrificing, dependable, generous, and helpful to others are generally of greater importance. Yet only those who fit the bill of "normal" are allowed full access to the individualistic qualities that such cultures value most. In other words, wealthy white men are expected to be independent, assertive, and self-reliant while others (women, people of color, people with disabilities, etc.) face harsh double standards.

There are some problems with these individualistic values to begin with—one is that they leave little space for true well-being and they can exacerbate anxiety. To be well, we need to feel and express our emotions. Well-being requires that we ask for help, build healthy relationships, and allow ourselves to depend on one another. Rugged individualism asks us to deny our vulnerability and prioritize appearing like we're okay over actually being okay. It also creates the misperception that people who appear happy and successful have achieved their success all on their own, without considering the impact of systemic factors like race, gender, class, and more.

Being well can be messy. In that messiness is our humanity, which is not sterile and controllable; it is vibrant, dynamic, shadowy, and light. When certain ways of being are normalized, and everything else is seen as a pathology or an aberration from this "normal," it harms the people who don't fit into those boxes—which is most of us. Plus, the box of "normal" even harms those who *do* fit in it. It reduces them to the qualities that are valued in society while denying the parts of them that aren't. For me, well-being isn't about striving to achieve "normalcy"; rather, the goal should be to gain a sense of resilience and inner stability that allow us to embrace what life gives us, feel joyful and connected, and have a rich inner life. Our ability to be with the complexity of what it means to be human is key.

Complexity and Stability

Systems theory is the interdisciplinary study of how systems function. One idea in this body of work is that complex systems are more stable than simple systems. Imagine a table with three legs. This is a simple system. If just one leg is broken, or loose or unstable, the whole system can fall apart. Now imagine a table with twenty legs. It can have several loose or broken legs without compromising its stability. It doesn't need every leg to be perfectly stable in order to be stable overall. This stability is something we can cultivate in ourselves.

Children have very simple emotional systems. They are usually only able to be aware of one feeling at a time. When they are having that emotion, it can feel like it will never change and has always been there. This is why when kids are upset about something, they tend to say things like, "you *never* let me . . ." and "she is *always* mean to me." Children haven't yet developed the brain capacity to have a strong feeling while knowing that it will likely change. The three parts of their brain (the rational higher brain, the emotional midbrain, and the impulsive lower brain, as discussed in chapter 1) are not connected yet. This is why children, all the way through adolescence, can be so emotional and impulsive—the lower brain centers are not yet fully connected to the rational higher brain centers. I can remember what it was like when I was an adolescent. Everything was so dramatic! My emotions felt like a life sentence, and when I was upset it was difficult to believe that I would eventually be okay. I have journals filled with dark poetry about heartbreak and pain. I was generally a happy child, but if you read my diaries, you'd find very little evidence of that.

As we mature (hopefully) we're able to have a difficult feeling while simultaneously knowing it's temporary and that we'll be okay. This allows us to tolerate that feeling without overly reacting to it. We are also able to have several different feelings at the same time (e.g., "I'm happy and scared" or "I'm glad you're here but I'm mad at you"). Trauma can get in the way of this brain growth, but because of neuroplasticity and the brain's capacity to change throughout our lifetime, we can change our brains and build new neural pathways and more robust connections between the different areas of our brains. The practices I'm sharing with you do just that!

Yoga is one of my favorite ways to work with adolescents whose brains may need support building these connections (that's all adolescents, by the way). Alonso, an eighth grader, attended a yoga class I taught at his school for a semester. He struggled with anxiety, which he experienced as irritation that would cause him to lose his temper often. He shared openly that he worried about his safety and his family's security living in a neighborhood plagued by violence and economic instability. He couldn't see a way out of his situation and it made him mad. I often started and ended class by asking the students to share how they felt with two or three words. On one particular day, Alonso's initial words were "angry and agitated," and by the end of the class his words were "angry and calm." This was pivotal because Alonso being able to feel angry and calm would serve him more in his life than being happy and calm. I want him to be happy, of course, but being able to hold competing feelings is an important form of self-regulation. If Alonso can learn to be with his anger without acting out, he'll have a better chance at working through the fear and anxiety beneath it, and he'll be less likely to act out and get himself into trouble.

Part of feeling regulated is being able to be with seemingly conflicting emotions and sensations at the same time. If we only ever feel all good or all bad, we don't have the capacity to hold the complexity of what it often means to be human. Practicing somatic tools like grounding and feeling your body can help you cultivate this ability to tolerate discomfort without getting overwhelmed or reactive. These are things you can do in the moment when unpleasant emotions emerge, and when you practice using such tools daily, they become easier to access during challenging moments. This is called resourcing ourselves; it's about building our capacity to be with discomfort.

Finding Resources

Self-regulation resources are tools that can help us be with uncomfortable emotions or sensations without being overwhelmed. They are like a flotation device we can hold on to if we find ourselves in tumultuous waters. Without the device we'd be flailing just to keep our heads above water. With the device, we are more able to get our bearings and assess the situation, see where the waves are coming from, and if there is a way to get to safety. Resources are things that we can hold on to (metaphorically and even literally) so that we can be with our experience without running away or drowning in it. I've discussed a few somatic practices that can be resources—things like grounding, centering, breathing and orienting. Now let's consider a broader range of resources.

When we're overwhelmed we don't have the wherewithal to take stock of our emotions, sensations, and impulses. We're just trying to survive and manage. However, when we have a resource, we can begin the process of addressing our unease and shifting it. A resource can be anything. It can be an object—a stone, crystal, candle, picture, tree—that you touch or imagine in moments of anxiety or overwhelm. A resource can be a smell that you seek out when you want to pause and focus. I'm partial to rose or lavender oil, myself, but I had a client once who used the smell of a pastrami sandwich on rye to get through a cesarean section during the birth of her baby. The most empowering resources are internal—practices like grounding, centering, orienting to present time, and breathing. All of these things can help us move out of overwhelm so we can be with our emotions and sensations and shift them. Resources don't cure us on their own; rather, they can support us in getting regulated enough to be able to handle difficulty. A crystal or stone offers weight and can be grounding, for example. Pausing to take a deep breath can allow us to find space for our feelings. Rocking our body can give us a sense of rhythm when things feel out of rhythm. We are often resourcing ourselves without even realizing it. What things are resources for you?

When we are not resourced, we're more likely to be reactive in stressful situations. When we are not resourced, we feel dysregulated—anxious, overwhelmed, depressed, scattered, and so forth. We are drowning in our experience. My favorite resource is grounding—the first practice I shared in chapter 1. Try it again right now: Notice your feet on the ground, your butt in the chair, or any part of your body that's connected to something touching the ground. Push your feet into the floor a bit so you feel your legs, or press your back against the chair. You might notice that your breath deepens or something settles. Don't worry if you don't; there are lots of resources and not all of them need to work for you.

When we are resourced, we are able to be responsive rather than reactive. We feel we have some choice over how we feel and how we act. We can grab on to our metaphorical safety device so that we can get a sense of the current and how to get out of the tumultuous water to safety.

Stress + no resource = Reactive behavior + dysregulation

Stress + resource = Responsive behavior + self-regulation

RESOURCING VISUALIZATION

Imagine a moderately stressful situation that you've experienced—nothing too overwhelming. As you think about this scenario, notice your sensations, emotions, and impulses. Name them to yourself and note their level of intensity. Don't rush this; take your time noticing what arises in you. Then pick a resource to work with (grounding, breath, or a smell, for example). Place at least half of your attention on your resource, and then track your sensations, emotions, and impulses while staying connected to your resource. If that's hard, go back and forth from your resource to whatever else you are feeling. Notice if the intensity or quality of what you are feeling shifts for the better when you're able to hold both the resource and the stressor in your awareness.

Tolerating Discomfort

When we are dysregulated, we can get fixated on one unpleasant aspect of our experience. We feel one cue of anxiety, and suddenly we are hyperfocused on it, fueling it with our attention and fear. But what if you felt the sensation of anxiety and then felt your feet on the floor, or your hands on your body, or took a deep breath? What if the anxiety became only one of the things you are feeling, rather than the only thing? When we are having a feeling that we don't like or are afraid of, we can sometimes give it all of our attention and miss cues of other things going on that could balance out our experience or help us be with it rather than being overwhelmed by it or running away.

Resources that help us tolerate discomfort and hold complex feelings can have a profound impact on our well-being. Eileen, a sixty-five-year-old woman, came to see me because she had been having panic attacks weekly for ten years. She explained that it all began when her husband had a heart attack and died. She was with him when this happened. Since then she'd had perpetual tightness in her chest, which eventually led to panic attacks. She understood that this was related to her experience of the death of her husband, but this knowledge didn't make her panic attacks go away.

During our session, I helped Eileen get resourced. She was naturally pretty grounded, and it wasn't hard for her to connect to her legs and a feeling of presence in the room. I asked her to describe the sensation in her chest. She said it was tension and that the emotion there was terror. Then I told her to let herself feel the terror/tension as she felt her feet on the floor (grounding). As she did that, she took a deep breath, and her shoulders dropped about an inch. She reported feeling tingling go down her arms (discharge of energy). Her body continued to settle, and she left feeling very relaxed. When she came back the following week, she was incredulous because she hadn't had a panic attack that week, for the first time in a decade. She asked why, and I explained that all she needed was to let her body know that she could feel the terror now.

You see, at the time of her husband's heart attack and death, Eileen had resisted feeling her terror because it was too much, and she had to deal with the crisis. Each time she'd tapped into the sensation or even her memory of that terror since then, her body/mind felt that it meant something awful was happening and that she should mobilize for an emergency. This impulse to avoid the tension and go into a fight-or-flight response became the source of her stress and panic attacks. Now that she was out of the stressful event, she could feel the terror and thus let it go. Essentially, we had to give her body the memo that there was no more danger and it could let go of the terror. By connecting to her resource, Eileen could be with the terror without running away from it; this allowed all the energy that was stuck to release its grip on her.

As we can tolerate our feelings and get more regulated, we are also able to experience more nuance and range in our emotional repertoire. We start to better distinguish between anger and sadness or jealousy and irritation. We might find new shades of joy, delight, and bliss. Rather than emotions feeling like black-and-white experiences that are very distinct and jagged, we can feel a greater sense of flow and variety in a way that adds depth and color to life. In the animated film *Inside Out*, this is expressed when the main character's emotional control center transforms as she matures. At first it only had a few discreet emotions on it, represented by four or five blocks of color. Then, after she gets to the other side of her big challenge and adventure, the new control center is covered in dozens of colors and shades and less discreet blocks.

ACCEPTANCE PRACTICE

Find a comfortable seated position. Start by finding something that feels good or supportive in your body or in the room. It can be your feet on the floor, your bottom in your chair, your back against a wall; it can be your breath or a candle; it can be an object that you hold in your hand. Anchoring your awareness in this resource, start to notice other sensations, emotions, or images that might emerge. Each time you notice something, say, "And this too I shall include." Then softly move on and see what comes up next. If you feel overwhelmed or you find your mind wandering (which it will do), simply focus again on finding something that feels supportive in your body or in your surroundings. I suggest doing this for about five minutes.

Building emotional complexity means that we don't need everything to be exactly perfect to feel okay. We are able to go with the flow. We are able to include and accept what life brings us without needing to control all of it.

Releasing Stress and Trauma

As discussed previously, life often requires us to remain regulated and not act on our impulses. Sometimes the impulses are inappropriate—you probably don't want to actually punch your boss or scream at the annoying person taking a long time at the grocery store checkout. Sometimes it's simply not safe to act on our impulses even if they are appropriate—if we're not able to fight back when being assaulted or if speaking our truth could get us arrested or fired, for example. This is why it is important to make sure we are releasing and discharging stress energy from our body, not just regulating it. If we don't, this energy will accumulate over time. Some of us are carrying this energy from our childhood, which is a time when we are more vulnerable to stress and trauma. Some of us are experiencing chronic stress from external circumstances like poverty, marginalization, or discrimination. Most of us are also carrying this energy from stressful events that we never fully recovered from later on in life.

When we have unresolved childhood trauma or even just too much unprocessed stress from our past, our nervous systems may feel more easily overloaded by common daily stressors. The discharge techniques I'm offering can be done regardless of the source of your trauma, but if you do know or suspect you have experienced some heavy stuff, don't try to work through deeper trauma all alone. Seek support from a professional so that you don't get overwhelmed.[5] It's kind of like starting to tidy up a messy house. The basic stuff we can do alone but getting deep into the corners and under the furniture requires more heavy-duty tools and support.

To discharge energy, we need to use our resources a bit differently than we do when we're working to regulate our emotions to prevent overwhelm or overreacting. When we're using resources to manage our feelings during a challenging experience, we are not necessarily releasing the energy that is bubbling up. Later, when we have more time, space, and safety, we can use these same resources to discharge and release the energy more fully. Here's an example from my life. A few years ago, I was leading a weeklong workshop in Florida with two other facilitators who I'd been working with for years. On my way to the afternoon session, I drove past a bad car accident. Out of the corner of my eye, I saw what looked like a dead body on the side of the road. It was very upsetting, and I felt my whole body get hot and tremble a bit. When I got to the workshop the group was already assembled, so I sat down next to one of my cofacilitators, who was leading the first thirty minutes, after which I would be giving a lecture. She often runs about ten minutes late with her piece, but it still gives me ample time to get through my lecture. I noticed that this time, as soon as she was running just one minute late, I started to get really irritated and annoyed at her. As I tracked my body, I could tell that this was the energy from seeing the car accident, not stress about running late. I was able to get regulated by planting my feet on the floor and focusing on my breath. This helped me to manage my activated nervous system and stay grounded until she finished, only eight minutes late. During my entire lecture I could feel the anxiety in my chest as tightness and constriction.

I had to work extra hard to manage it so I could get through my lecture smoothly.

That evening, when we got back to our hotel, I told my cofacilitators what I had seen and how shocking the experience had been. At first the anxiety got stronger; now that I wasn't managing it in order to hold space for others, the feelings came in full force. I reminded myself that my friends were there to support me, and I tried to stay connected to my breath and feel my feet on the floor. These resources (connection with friends, grounding, and breathing) allowed me to stay with the feelings rather than try to manage them again. I shed a few tears, felt my legs tremble a bit, and, after a few minutes, the intensity dissipated. I sensed my body release the energy of terror, shock, and fear. Suddenly I was exhausted. I felt like I had run an emotional marathon, so I took a warm bath and went to bed. I woke up the next morning feeling refreshed and energized; the experience was behind me, and I was ready for a new day of teaching.

During this experience, I used my resources first to manage my anxiety so I could do what I needed to do in the moment, which was not get unnecessarily angry and give a coherent lecture. Later, when I had the space, I used my tools to let myself feel and release. Releasing pent-up energy does not have to be dramatic. Sometimes it can feel great to just scream to get it out, but other times small releases can be powerful too. In my training in Somatic Experiencing I was taught that "small is big." I was taught to titrate the release of energy so that it can really be integrated; in other words, it can sometimes be greatly beneficial to release energy bit by bit rather than all at once. You may have learned about titration in chemistry class—when combining water and hydrochloric acid, for example, if you quickly pour the acid into the water it can cause a strong reaction and overflow. But if you slowly drip the acid into the solution, it is integrated and neutralized without too strong of a reaction. So, for example, if you want to release the energy associated with not being able to speak your truth, instead of screaming really loud, you might hum in a low tone a few times. This smaller action can sometimes be integrated more fully rather than a dramatic response that may throw your system into overwhelm. Discharge can often feel like a tingling, settling, or even a temperature change. Sometimes you'll yawn, or your belly will gurgle. These can all be signs that your nervous system is releasing and settling.

DISCHARGE PRACTICE WITH SOUND

Take a few moments to get grounded and resourced. You can sit still, or allow your body to rock if that feels regulating. Then start to make some low humming sounds with your lips gently pressed together. You can put a hand on your heart and feel the vibration of your hum there. For extra grounding, put one hand on the floor as you hum. If emotions arise, stay resourced and allow them to flow through you if it's not overwhelming. You can do this for three to five minutes.

It's usually best to allow discharge to happen slowly. Sometimes, however, if we feel really stuck and we are grounded enough, more intense and cathartic experiences can be helpful. If you have a hard time tapping into your feelings, you may need those types of experiences to help you connect to what's going on deep inside of you.

Daily Maintenance

Many of us have some work to do around releasing energy from past traumas. But we also need to release and discharge energy that accumulates from our daily life. It's like cleaning up as you go along—you may know that there's work to do under the bed and in the attic, but you still want to pick up your socks and wipe down the countertops. This translates into not waiting for things to get extreme before you attend to them. It means doing things to regulate yourself throughout your day, so stress doesn't build up unnecessarily. Many of us wait until we have a crisis to attend to our self-care. We override our body's signals until it's speaking to us so loudly that we can't deny it. Some of us pride ourselves on our ability to endure. It makes us feel strong and useful. Plus, what would we do with ourselves if we weren't struggling? Who would we be?

A daily practice of releasing stress can go a long way. This requires interoception and a willingness to pause and reflect. It requires us to have empathy and patience for ourselves and to understand that our nervous system doesn't always behave reasonably but we still need to attend to it. Sometimes self-care requires us to be really honest with ourselves—we may need to recognize that maintaining our well-being means prioritizing our needs over our desire to meet other peoples' needs and expectations. It might even mean disappointing others.

Last year my family took up downhill skiing. My husband grew up skiing, and he loves it. I grew up in Florida, and the idea of hurling my body down a snowy mountain does not feel like a good idea at all. I wanted to give it a try because I knew my kids would love it—which they did—and I thought it could be a fun family activity.

The first few times I skied, my body felt like I was falling uncontrollably down a mountain. I seriously hated it! My husband kept commenting that I was actually doing a great job and learning fast. Regardless, my nervous system, having no prior experience with skiing, didn't buy it. I was in a state of fight-or-flight the whole day. My cognitive mind knew that many people actually enjoy the experience of skiing, but all I saw around me when I was on the slopes were signs of danger. I watched reasonable adults put skis on small children and encourage them to go down the mountain. I saw older people skiing with total confidence and competence. I felt like I was in a sci-fi movie where no one realized how much danger everyone was actually in except me.

I kept trying, over and over again, to keep up with my husband and kids. And I did. But I didn't for one second enjoy it. I dreaded every twist and turn. I was gripping my entire being the whole way, and by the time I'd get to the bottom of a run, I was sweating and my legs were cramping. Everyone else, on the other hand, was cheerful and happy. Finally I realized that even though I had acquired the skills to do the intermediate slopes, I needed to stick to the easier ones in order to make it through the day without being overwhelmed. (I remembered to let my knowledge of stress and nervous system regulation guide my learning process, duh!) I chose to ski the easy slopes until my nervous system could catch up with my cognitive mind, which knew skiing could be fun. Not pushing as hard as I could was a little bit embarrassing, and I was tempted to try and keep up with everyone again to prove that I wasn't a total wimp, but I knew that if I continued to overwhelm myself I'd never find the joy in skiing that others swear by or, worse, I'd get hurt.

Many of us learn our lessons the hard way. We spend years overriding our body's signals. We power through until we can't anymore. Sometimes this is because there's no other choice—there's no chance to rest or get the support we need. Sometimes it's because we're just not listening or we take pride in working hard and burning out. When we do this, we can make ourselves sick—physically and emotionally. And we're not so great to be around, either.

Addicted to Stress?

Many of us get used to battling a certain level of stress, which can sometimes lead us to unconsciously maintain that level of stress because it is what we are used to. In an ideal world, we would all have just the right amount of stress that suited our temperaments. Some people can thrive on a fast pace (as long as they are also able to decompress and relax), while others need a slower pace. I've worked with many people who, when they get really honest with themselves, admit that they are afraid of not being distracted by their stress. Being calm actually scares them! Like Ana.

Ana had a consistent habit of rushing. Anytime she had to be somewhere at a specific time, she would find herself rushing and arriving just on time or a few minutes late. She overcommitted herself in general and never felt like she had enough time for anything. Ana's partner Alex moved at a much slower pace. He didn't like to pack his schedule and he always arrived at appointments five or ten minutes early. He liked to take his time. When Ana and Alex had to be somewhere together, the difference in how they paced their lives became obvious. Alex would be ready to leave the house to be on time or early; Ana was never ready when Alex was. Just as it was time to leave, Ana would decide to quickly throw in a load of laundry or return a few more emails.

Ana always tried to squeeze in as many tasks as she could. She enjoyed the feeling of having accomplished a lot, and she found the stress and rushing exciting. Yet her fast pace had a detrimental effect as well—she had insomnia and chronic stomachaches. When she married Alex, she realized that when they went to appointments early, on his rhythm, she could barely tolerate the stillness of waiting for five or ten minutes. She would get anxious when she wasn't rushing. Plus, sitting around for ten minutes felt like a waste of time! I recommended that Ana start meditating—just for one or two minutes a day, to start, so she could learn to tolerate stillness. It was hard for her, and she realized that one of her formative experiences as a child could be behind some of her impulse to rush. When Ana was twelve, her family escaped El Salvador because it had become too unsafe. They traveled all the way to Mexico by foot and in crowded vans and crossed the US border illegally in the middle of the night. Eventually Ana was able to become a US citizen, but the experience of her family's escape lived in her, and she never felt like she could be still. During their journey, letting her guard down for even a moment could have gotten everyone in trouble. To this day, being still made her anxious, even though she technically had no reason to be on the run.

Meditation helped Ana recalibrate her nervous system so that it didn't associate stillness with danger. Taking a few minutes to pause was very uncomfortable, but slowly she could tolerate it more and more, and eventually it even started to feel good. As she got more comfortable with stillness, she was able to shift her pace and slow down a bit. Ana never reached Alex's level of mellow, but she did find a pace that was more sustainable for her. She started sleeping better and her stomachaches went away. Her movements were no longer an avoidance of stillness, and this made all the difference in her well-being.

REFLECTION

What is your relationship to stress? Who would you be if you weren't stressed? Is there anything scary about the concept of not being stressed out?

Shifting Our Limiting Beliefs

One factor that can keep us trapped in our stress and anxiety is our unconscious need to feel that our beliefs about the world are accurate. Most of us would rather be right than feel good, and we would rather deal with what is familiar than risk the unknown. I had a client, Helena, who hated her job. She was a graphic designer at a small firm. She had been with the company for five years and disliked the nature of her work, most of her coworkers, and the environment she was in. Helena was good at her job. Over the years, she had received several offers at other firms that looked promising. But each time she found some reason to stay in her current situation. As she explored this, she realized that there was safety in her current job that she was afraid to lose. At her current job, everything was predictable. She knew how to deal with her moody boss and her irritating coworkers. She was attached to the predictability of her situation. She got to be right each time what she expected to happen happened. Even though she was unhappy, there was a security in knowing what to expect. In a new situation, even a better one, she would have to face the unknown—and that was scary.

Some of us don't know our way around a life without our familiar suffering. We unconsciously choose to recreate our same flavor of suffering because we have become experts at dealing with it. We also may not recognize when there is evidence that contradicts what we expect. This is called *confirmation bias*. Not only do we tend to see evidence that confirms what we already believe and not register things that don't, we tend to set things up so that they occur in a way that confirms our beliefs, even if it means we are disappointed!

One of my limiting beliefs is that I have to do everything on my own—no one is capable of helping me, nor do I deserve the support. (This is a common one, especially for people who had to play the role of helper in their family of origin.) In order to shift this, I had to start taking some risks that included asking for help. This terrified me. One day, I was running late to meet my husband at our kids' school for parent-teacher conferences. I needed to get their bag of snacks from the house, which was out of the way. Instead of going there myself, I decided to ask Paul to do it as a way to practice asking for help. When I called to ask him, he said he'd be happy to do it. Then I asked him to feed the dog and throw a load of laundry into the machine, without being late. When we met up at the school, he had done everything except the laundry because there wasn't enough time. I noticed myself feeling self-righteous and relieved. He had confirmed my belief that no one else can help me. I had set him up to fail so I could have my limiting belief affirmed. There was no urgency around the laundry at all, yet I chose to add it to his list—knowing, subconsciously, that he wouldn't have the time to complete that task. Our beliefs can be a self-fulfilling prophecy.

It can be tricky to uncover our limiting beliefs. They are often so ingrained in us that they just feel like reality; like the waters we are swimming in. One way to begin to reveal these unconscious beliefs is to reflect on some of the patterns in your life regarding relationships, work, money, stability, and your self-worth. For a moment, consider that many of the situations in your life may be influenced by your own expectations. For example, let's say you believe that most people are not to be trusted, and you have solid evidence for this. Consider that maybe this belief of yours either draws you toward people who will let you down or colors your perception so that you see and feel evidence that validates your fear. Not everything is a result of our beliefs, of course, but in order to examine what might be, this mental reflection can be useful. Use the exercises below to explore what your own limiting beliefs might be.

REFLECTION: DISCOVERING YOUR LIMITING BELIEFS

Without thinking about it too much, complete the following sentences:

1. People are _____.

2. I deserve _____.

3. When it comes to my work, I _____.

4. In order to be loved, I _____.

5. My body is _____.

6. My deepest fear is _____.

7. One thing I know for sure is _____.

8. Compared to other people, I _____.

REFLECTION: SHIFTING YOUR LIMITING BELIEFS

As you review your answers to the previous reflection, write down one or two limiting beliefs that you may carry. Notice how they feel in your body when you reflect on them. Then, for each belief, write down its opposite. You don't need to believe it, just try it on and see how it feels. It will probably make you uncomfortable—that's good! Spend time reflecting on these new thoughts about yourself and the world—perhaps journal about them or recite one every day as an affirmation. Consider how shifting your beliefs could serve you in the future.

When Shifting Our Beliefs Is Not Enough

Changing our beliefs can sometimes genuinely change our reality. I wish it were always that simple, but unfortunately some of us are actually more likely to encounter certain difficulties than others. Some of us are targets in the world based only on who we are—how we look or express ourselves, what we believe, or other core aspects of who we are. The impacts of discrimination and oppressions like racism, sexism, classism, ableism, homophobia, transphobia, fatphobia, religious bias, and more are real. Often people from targeted groups are accused of being overly sensitive when they name their experiences and others' biases, but this vigilance usually comes from a lived experience that people who are not in their position simply can't see. This vigilance can show up unnecessarily, of course, but it's important to not assume that we all have the same capacity to shift our beliefs and then see such shifts reflected back to us in the world. It's also important to note that for every act of discrimination or harm that is pointed out, there are likely innumerable others that pass without comment, though likely not without an impact on someone's life.

My friend Bryonn Bain is an example of this. Bryonn was class president for the four years I was at Columbia University. He is a meditator, a vegan, and a charismatic, passionate person. He is also Black. So when Bryonn was walking through Harlem not far from campus, it didn't matter that he had a strong sense of self-worth when the police arrested him and his cousins because the officers thought they looked like people who had committed a crime nearby. To the police, he was just a Black man who looked suspicious. Even when Bryonn clearly and calmly explained that he and his cousins were just walking home from a party, it made no difference. The arresting officers didn't believe that these three young men with no prior arrest records were innocent. It was not their limiting beliefs that caused their arrest and poor treatment from law enforcement, it was the limiting beliefs of a society that cannot imagine that three Black men are innocent, upstanding citizens. Eventually Bryonn and his cousins were able to prove their innocence and not face prison time. Bryonn has gone on to make his life's work as a lawyer and an artist to address racial profiling and wrongful incarceration.

For people who are targets in the world simply because of their identities, it is especially difficult but also important to do the work of shifting limiting beliefs. Internalizing the toxic messages we get about our bodies and our existence doubles their harm and traps us even further. When the world hasn't shown us much evidence that we are safe, loveable, and worthy, it can be very hard to recognize it or trust that the opposite is actually true. Refusing to internalize messages of oppression is a powerful act of resistance that allows us to love ourselves and others even as social and economic oppression impacts us. As Audre Lorde once wrote, "Caring for myself is not self-indulgence, it is self-preservation, and that is an act of political warfare."[6] She reminds us that our personal sense of worth is impacted by broader systemic issues like politics and culture.

REFLECTION

Do you come from a group that is currently or has been historically marginalized, minimized, or oppressed? If so, have you internalized beliefs and judgments about yourself and your community based on this? What are these beliefs? Go back and do the previous reflection with these beliefs if you haven't already.

For everyone, whether you come from a marginalized group or not: Have you internalized assumptions or judgments about people who come from these groups? Be honest about what groups and what the specific assumptions are. In what way might you unwittingly be contributing to the anxiety of others from these groups?

Well-Being

Well-being can mean many things to different people. When we are well, we feel content, happy, and grounded. We also allow ourselves to feel anger, grief, sadness, and fear. Life feels meaningful and purposeful, and we can trust its ebbs and flows. Being well means we are integrated, and we don't need to deny any parts of ourselves. We are not encumbered by shame, and we can accept who we are and, in turn, accept others for who they are. We trust that we can get through most difficulties that may lie ahead. When we are well we are not constantly looking for things outside of us to make us happy, and we are able to be in meaningful and healthy relationships. We are able to move beyond surviving into thriving.

REFLECTION
What does well-being mean to you? Write in a stream-of-consciousness way for a few minutes and/or draw an image.

Being well is not completely in our individual control. Some people may not have the opportunity to experience all the things I just listed. This is why true well-being has to include a consciousness about how we might contribute to a world where everyone has a chance to be well.

4

Transforming Trauma

The Gift in the Wound

INVESTIGATING THE IMPACT of trauma in our lives can be an important part of healing our anxiety. Unresolved traumatic experiences from our past can fuel (and be the source of) our anxiety, unbeknownst to us. Sometimes people don't realize that some of the experiences they have had may have been traumatic and could be the root causes of their suffering.

As a trauma survivor, trauma therapist, and trauma-informed yoga teacher working with survivors for almost two decades, I have many thoughts on the topic of healing trauma. I have worked with people who have endured the unimaginable. I have seen people triumph over trauma and come out better on the other side of it, people become trapped in the grasp of trauma unable to come out, and everything in between. Ultimately, I believe that we can all find some healing from trauma, and, with the right information and support, let ourselves be transformed by it in a meaningful way. As my teacher Peter Levine says, "Trauma is a fact of life, but it doesn't have to be a life sentence." He goes on to say, "I believe not only that trauma is curable, but that the healing process can be a catalyst for profound awakening."[1] When I think of trauma, I don't just think of the negative impacts of it,

I also think about the ways we grow and learn when have to deal with overwhelming situations. My intention is not to bypass the pain and horror that trauma can inflict on people, but I also don't want to bypass peoples' resilience and capacity.

In my presentations on trauma, I often show a slide of a diamond and a piece of coal, with the phrase, "A diamond is just a piece of coal that handled stress exceptionally well." It is only by being exposed to the stress of extreme heat and pressure that the coal can transform. The stress of life shapes us as well, yet none of us are perfect diamonds—we have parts that are shiny, parts that are broken, parts still covered in coal. Trauma shapes us. As we reflect on this, please keep in mind both ends of the healing process—the coal and the diamond—and the spectrum in between. It's important to consider what has shaped you and its implications for who you are today. I also want you to reflect on how trauma might have impacted those around you. If the pain is fresh, deep, or in any way overwhelming, I encourage you to seek the support of a therapist. It's not always appropriate to work with trauma on one's own; you deserve support!

REFLECTION

If you were born into the world as a raw piece of coal, what are the life experiences that shaped you into who you are today and who you see yourself being tomorrow? Consider answering in a stream-of-consciousness style or in poetry.

In chapter 1, I defined trauma as anything that overwhelms our capacity to cope and respond and leaves us feeling helpless, hopeless, and out of control. As I mentioned before, it is not the event itself that is traumatic, it's our response to it that determines if it was traumatic or not. Not all trauma comes from what most people would consider a major experience—some traumas are what we might call "little t" traumas (as opposed to "big T" Traumas). "Little t" traumas may not be as major, but they can overwhelm us and shape us nonetheless. I often share that I have "hair trauma." I say this not to joke about trauma but to share that even seemingly small experiences we have can have a significant impact. You see, I have very frizzy hair. I grew up in Miami, Florida, which has 100 percent humidity most of the time. My mom used to cut my hair. She is not a professional hairdresser. I had short hair that just seemed to puff around my head like a disheveled mass no matter what I did. This may not sound overwhelming, but to an adolescent girl, where concerns around peer group acceptance feel like life or death, it certainly is! Coupled with being an immigrant and feeling like an outsider, my hair preoccupied me for most of my adolescence. I was never part of the popular group of kids, and I often felt excluded and judged. This experience shaped my identity, and to this day there's still a part of me that feels like I don't fit in.

I think about trauma in three categories: shock, developmental, and systemic. We are all shaped by at least one of these categories. We can experience "big T" or "little t" traumas in each. Sometimes we don't realize that certain things are traumatic because the traumatic experience is all we know and we don't have the perspective to realize that our experience may be out of the ordinary. As you read through the next sections, reflect on your own life experience and what has shaped you. Remember, just because a lot of bad stuff might have happened to you doesn't mean you are traumatized. If you had good resources and support, you may have been buffered against the negative impact.

Shock Trauma

Shock traumas are events that happen to us. These are things like car accidents, medical trauma, experiencing or witnessing violence, natural disasters, divorce, and the death of loved ones. These events can overwhelm us and when they do, we defend, dissociate, or find other strategies to cope as best we can. (The possum being chased by the fox in chapter 1 experienced a shock trauma.) When something happens that we can't cope with and respond to, it can cause us to go into a freeze or collapse state. These are both protective mechanisms that our bodies use to try and keep us safe. Freeze is a rigid immobility response. People can experience this after a car accident or in the face of a threat that they can't deal with. Once the event is over, if they're not able to discharge the energy from the body, it can get "stuck" and impact them indefinitely. They might find themselves panicky and on high alert each time they're in a car, or constantly worried that something bad is about to happen.

The collapse response is similar to freeze but looks a bit different. Collapse is a shutting-down experience. (Remember the ON/OFF graph? It's the OFF part.) Collapse is common with sexual trauma. It's a survival strategy: if someone is doing something to your body that you don't want but feel powerless to stop, one of the most protective things you can do is shut down and leave your body so you don't feel anything. This is an involuntary reflex—it's not something one chooses to do. Often sexual trauma survivors feel ashamed because they may not have done anything to stop the abuse. This is because they froze or collapsed. Their nervous system got overwhelmed and, to protect them, shut down all feeling. Collapse is necessary at the time yet becomes a problem when it's happening in situations that are not necessarily traumatic.

I had a client who experienced molestation by a family member as a child. (This is a shock trauma that was chronic and repeated.) When it was happening, she would "fall asleep," which was a collapse response that allowed her to dissociate from the abuse. As an adult, she found that if she was in situations that became physically intimate, she would get spacey and leave her body only to realize later that she had engaged in a sexual experience without actually consenting to it. In some cases she wanted to be intimate, in others she didn't, but mostly she was confused. She didn't have the embodied awareness to know what she wanted in order to make an empowered choice. It was as if her internal GPS would just turn off in intimate situations.

Conversation around "enthusiastic consent" is so important in order to ensure that all parties in a sexual situation are fully present and truly want each step of the interaction. Sexual assault survivors may not always be vocal about whether they want sexual intimacy or not, and people can take advantage of that, both knowingly and unknowingly. True consent should be active and positive, it's not just the absence of saying no. As my client worked through her trauma, she was able to stay grounded and present when in intimate situations. Rather than dissociating, she used the self-regulation resources that she practiced using during our sessions to stay present in her body when on a date. Grounding was especially important for her. Then she was able to start setting boundaries and vocalize what she needed and wanted. Much of her work was done when she found a supportive partner who was familiar and safe. He supported her by checking in consistently when they were being intimate to make sure she was comfortable. He encouraged her to set boundaries and ask for what she wanted, and he was patient when she didn't know what she wanted and needed time to figure it out.

Developmental Trauma

Another source of trauma does not have to do with a specific event but rather results from our relationships with a primary caretaker. Developmental trauma occurs when there is an ongoing misattunement with one's primary caretaker. A vital part of healthy childhood development is feeling cared for and responded to by our caretaker—a parent, grandparent, or any other caring adult. For example, an infant's cries should ideally be responded to with warmth and a desire to assess and meet the baby's need. Most babies have very basic needs—food, comfort, and safety. Humans are born 100 percent dependent on their caretakers for survival for years, so attunement is literally a life-or-death need. For most other animals, this isn't the case. A baby horse, for example, can walk within two hours of birth and is able to eat on its own within two weeks. It doesn't rely on the mother for its sole sustenance and survival for too long.

Human babies can't do anything for themselves. If our basic needs aren't met fairly consistently or predictably, we can develop a sense that people and the world are unsafe, unpredictable, or unresponsive. This leaves a lasting imprint on us, and for many people with developmental trauma, it takes work to figure out how to be in a healthy relationship where their needs are met. Love and pain get coupled together, and people can find themselves drawn into unhealthy relationships with people who have similar traits to their original caretaker. Relationships end up being the cause of much pain and anxiety, yet they also can be the source of healing.

Healing developmental trauma has to happen in relationship. It can't just happen on the therapy couch or meditation cushion. We have to actually learn how to relate with others in a healthier way, and we can only learn that by being in relationships that give us the space to make mistakes safely—to "practice badly," so to speak. Whether it's learning a new language or learning how to ride a bike, gaining any new skill requires us to be willing and able to be bad at it before we can get good at it. This goes for relationships too. Working with a therapist can be the first step—the clear boundaries of a therapeutic relationship can create a low-stakes environment without too many unknown variables. The next step is to figure out how to translate that work into relationships outside of the therapy room. Marcia's story offers a good example.

Marcia grew up with a mother who was emotionally unstable and had bipolar disorder. As a baby, when Marcia would cry, her mother would shout at her that she was selfish and withdraw from her. Sometimes she would be left with a soiled diaper for hours. It didn't take too long for Marcia to stop crying altogether because it never yielded a good result. As she got older, she learned to avoid doing anything that might upset her mother. When she would do something that disturbed her mother, she would get screamed at or hit. For a toddler this is incredibly overwhelming, and Marcia became immobilized by her anxiety. She felt extremely ashamed anytime she committed something her mother saw as an indiscretion, even though most of these things were developmentally appropriate behaviors like wanting to be picked up, feeling scared at night, or making a mess. Marcia learned that her needs were an inconvenience and that her role was to meet her mother's needs. That was her imprint of what a relationship is that she carried into her adult life.

Inevitably, in her adult relationships Marcia had a very hard time finding mutually supportive friends and partners. She had no idea how to navigate having her own needs in relationships and was mostly focused on not upsetting the other person. She didn't know what behavior was acceptable and what wasn't, and she constantly second-guessed herself. Relationships of any kind made her feel anxious and overwhelmed. She also tended to be drawn to people who were emotionally unpredictable and volatile—they felt familiar and matched her original experience of what relationships are. Marcia had to work really hard to figure out both how to choose more stable people and how to show up in relationships in a healthier way. With the support of a skilled therapist who could offer consistency and warmth, she was able to explore her issues and get more clarity on the role she tends to play in relationships. She practiced communicating her needs and setting boundaries. Eventually, she was able to experience healthy mirroring and consistent warmth from her therapist, which began to give her the space to not feel so anxious while relating to another person. This was important because as she got more regulated, she could imagine approaching other relationships feeling more grounded and empowered in herself.

Her next step in healing was to practice, in very small ways, showing up differently in her existing relationships. She practiced setting boundaries and expressing her needs. Sometimes this would go well and the other person would respect the request, and sometimes it backfired and the other person would get angry and push back. She had to end some relationships with people who weren't able to participate in a healthy dynamic. She also began to look for healthier people to engage with. She started dating someone who was very different from the emotionally abusive men that were typically her type. Joel was warm and kind. Marcia wasn't initially attracted to him; in fact, she found him annoying. Her therapist gently reminded her that guys that were "her type" replicated her trauma. Maybe someone she didn't think she'd like would afford her a chance to shift her pattern and try something new. Marcia was able to express herself with Joel without anxiety. He was consistent and didn't lose control if Marcia did something that bothered him. He was the perfect person for Marcia to "practice badly" with. Ultimately Joel wasn't the right person for Marcia, but he was an important teacher because without his extra gentleness, she would not have been able to learn the things she needed in order to show up for her next relationship in a healthy way. Richard was a better match for Marcia. He had a stronger personality than Joel, but was kind as well. With Marcia's new confidence and self-awareness, she could be with someone like Richard without losing herself. But there would have been no Richard without Joel.

Eventually Marcia was able to understand that her mother was a trauma survivor who was doing the best she could with the tools she had. Marcia's mother was physically abused as a child. She was never attuned to herself, so she didn't know how to do that for Marcia. Because she didn't get the support she needed, she passed her trauma on to Marcia. This is one way that trauma gets passed on from generation to generation, as discussed earlier.

Parents don't have to be perfectly healed to be able to do a good job raising their kids. Donald Winnicott, a child psychologist, coined the term "the good enough mother."[2] He found in his research on attachment that although it is very important that children be attuned to and responded to, it is also important that they find age-appropriate ways to self-soothe and meet their own needs. He found that attunement need not be perfect; in fact, it's better if a child learns to deal with "manageable disappointments" at appropriate stages of development in order to feel their own sense of competency. So as you consider your own childhood, use caution and don't blame your parents for everything. And if you're a parent, don't feel like you have to do everything perfectly either! I have to admit, before having children of my own, when I would hear clients talk about some of the ways that their parents failed them, I felt a lot of judgment for the parents. Now that I'm a parent, when I hear stories of parents' shortcomings I have a lot more empathy. Being a parent is hard!

It's possible to feel that you have some development trauma even if you think that all your needs were met as a child. For example, if you had smothering or overly fearful caretakers, you may not have been given enough opportunity to experience your own resilience and independence. If we aren't given a chance to experience our own competency, the world can feel overwhelming and unmanageable. This tends to be more of an issue these days when some parents can track their children's every move on a cell phone and stay in touch with them twenty-four seven. The terms *helicopter parent* and *snowplow parent* have been used to describe how some modern parents tend to watch over their kids way too much (like a helicopter) and/or try and remove any potential obstacles from their children's path (like a snowplow). This is more possible for some families than others, of course; not all people have the same access or ability to overprotect their children in this way. Children need the right balance of challenge and protection to grow and thrive.

Systemic Trauma

Systemic trauma is caused by the overwhelm of having to deal with issues that stem from larger systems and institutions that are meant to care for us and protect us. These include health care, education, the criminal justice system, financial institutions, government, and culture, to name a few. Unfortunately, at least in the United States, these systems benefit some and harm many. Discrimination and oppression also become normalized by cultural beliefs and enforced through social norms and behaviors. Things like classism, ableism, racism, sexism, homophobia, transphobia, mental health stigma, and more are very, very stressful to the people on the receiving end.

One heartbreaking example of systemic shock trauma is police violence against Black people. The disproportionate killing of Black people by police is traumatic to the Black community, whether they have been directly involved in this violence or not. Black people are up to six times more likely to be fatally shot by law enforcement than white people.[3] They are more likely to be stopped by police and questioned and searched without reason. Many Black people have to maintain a constant hypervigilance when out in the world, whether they are anticipating the potential for violence from law enforcement or being perceived as a threat by non-Black people who may call law enforcement on them.

Black parents (and non-Black parents of Black children) worry constantly about the safety of their children. They have to have "the talk" with their children starting as early as age eight—about the fact that not all police officers are safe and, for example, that they cannot play with a toy gun because someone might think it is real (as in the case of Tamir Rice, a twelve-year-old Black boy who was playing with a toy gun by himself in a Cleveland park when he was fatally shot by an officer who claimed to have felt threatened by the boy after only two seconds on the scene). They often live in a constant, daily state of fear that they or their children could be hurt or killed by the very people who are supposed to protect them. If this is not your lived reality, take a moment to pause and sit with how this systemic experience of trauma might exacerbate a person's anxiety.

All the personal therapy and self-help books in the world are not going to let a Black parent feel totally safe with their child out in a world where they are targets. Most parents worry about their children already; having to worry that the systems that are allegedly put in place to help us might actually harm us is an added and overwhelming burden. That's the thing with systemic trauma: it can't be healed just with personal work. Personal work can help people cope with the stress, but until the laws, practices and culture change, people subject to identity-based violence will have to remain on high alert.

Systemic inequality and oppression can also result in developmental trauma. Consider these scenarios: A child is crying because she is scared, but no one comes to her aid because she is in an understaffed day care center since parents each have to work two minimum wage jobs just to make ends meet for the family. Or maybe the child is being shuffled through the foster care system because her single mom is in jail after being racially profiled for a crime she did not commit. In both of these scenarios, the parents may have the emotional capacity to attune to the child, but because of poverty, lack of societal investment in social supports like affordable day care, or racial injustice, they can't be there. What about a child who is raised as a boy but knows herself to be a girl? Maybe this child expresses very early on that she is a girl, but because her family doesn't understand what it means to be transgender, she is told that she is a boy and is discouraged from expressing feminine behaviors or preferences. Perhaps this is what the parents are told to do by psychologists and their pastor. In this example, the caregivers are trying to do the right thing, but inadvertently they are misattuning to their child.

For some people, the threat of systemic trauma might not be immediate physical threats but other types of threats to safety and well-being. Women get paid less than men for comparable work. Low-income people don't generally have access to good health care, housing, or schools. Black people are disproportionately arrested and incarcerated. People who are not citizens can be separated from their families and forced to leave the country without any notice. Transgender and gender nonconforming people don't always have a safe bathroom available to them or adequate health-care options. Formerly incarcerated people often become ineligible for low-income housing and other types of assistance. Many of those listed above are also at risk of being the victims of violence based on their identity.

These examples complicate a trauma framework that focuses simply on individual and familial psychology and reveal how systemic and cultural dynamics can impact people profoundly. Most of these scenarios are currently legal and thus upheld systemically and institutionally. It's legal to have only gendered bathrooms, for example. Until recently, sentencing laws were different for drugs typically used by people of color versus white people. Public schools are funded by property taxes, so schools in affluent areas get a lot more resources than schools in poor areas. Quality health care is expensive, and there are no laws that protect low-income people from inadequate health-care providers. Many of the things built into our policies and systems are a reflection or even a cause of cultural norms. Even when the laws change (like sentencing laws, for example) bias lingers in the culture, past harms and unfairness aren't necessarily addressed, and the dynamics don't necessarily improve.

It is important to note that systemic advantages and disadvantages are not earned. I did nothing to earn my light skin or the money I inherited from my parents, for example. Similarly, a transgender person does not "earn" getting harassed simply by walking down the street and a Black person does not "earn" a harsher sentence than a white person for the same offense.

If you find yourself getting defensive around these ideas, it could be because you benefit from these systems. It's often harder to see discrimination if it's not aimed at you. So please bear with me here if these ideas rile you up. Use the tools I've shared; notice your sensations, impulses, and emotions. Try to stay resourced so that you can be curious about your reaction and what it may reveal to you. Just because I might be implying that you benefit from these systems doesn't mean you haven't seriously struggled in your life. It also doesn't mean you created these unfair systems. And it doesn't mean that you don't benefit from one system while being oppressed by another.

Some people don't believe in the impacts of systemic trauma because they were able to get themselves out of poverty or a life of marginalization, crime, or addiction. They may have a hard time empathizing with those who don't have the same strength, determination, or opportunities. This sort of exceptionalism is tricky because it reaffirms the idea of the "American dream," which says that anyone can make it if they try hard enough. Some people certainly experience this, but, until the playing field is fair, the dream is deceptive. Research has shown that the idea that we live in a meritocracy—where anyone can succeed if they try—is a myth. I have immense respect for people who were able to create abundant, meaningful lives even if they grew up with very little opportunity, but I'm interested in a world where no one has to dig themselves out of a ditch in order to feel human or be treated with dignity. I want us to change the rule, not celebrate the exceptions to the rule.

Ultimately we are all harmed by systems of inequality in some way. This book was written in 2020, during the onset of the COVID-19 global pandemic. At the time of this writing, hundreds of thousands of people have died, tens of millions of people are unemployed in the US alone, and essential workers are risking their lives every day to keep the world running. Older people, people with disabilities, people of color, low-income people, and people without access to quality health care are being disproportionately impacted. Among other things, the pandemic is revealing that until the most vulnerable are cared for, no one can be safe. Unless we find a way to protect everyone, this virus will continue to spread. And until we find a way to take care of essential workers with adequate protection, health care, and paid sick leave, they will not be able to do their work, which provides the basic needs and infrastructure we all rely on. Many of these essential workers do work that is unseen and underappreciated—such as health-care workers and first responders, people in waste management, those who work in grocery stores and pharmacies, food production and agricultural workers, transportation and postal workers, people in manufacturing, and mental health providers.

Research shows that in countries with higher income inequality, *everyone* fares worse.[4] Plus, just knowing that some of the advantages many of us have come at the expense of others is psychologically disturbing. It takes a certain amount of denial to deal with that. I know each time I buy cheap clothing because it's what I can afford at the time, I feel guilty knowing the workers who made the clothes were probably not paid a fair wage. When my husband and I bought our first home, I felt conflicted owning land that was stolen from the Indigenous peoples who originally inhabited the area. Even though we donate money to the local Tongva tribe, I still sit with the discomfort being complicit in an unjust system.

REFLECTION

What has been the role of systemic trauma in your life? Where have you benefited from systems of inequality and where have you or your ancestors been disadvantaged by them? Consider your access to education, quality health care, job security, safety, clean air and water, healthy food, and housing as well as whether you have to deal with discrimination and/or oppression.

Reflection on the roles we play in systems of inequality as well as the ways we've internalized some of the values and messages they give us is one key to our collective healing from overwhelm and anxiety—how we can all heal together as a society, culture, and world. None of us alive today created the oppressive systems that surround us, but together we can change them so that everyone is treated with dignity and respect and has access to what they need. Call me an idealist, but I've dedicated my life to this goal. We may not see it in our lifetime, but we can be part of setting things into motion for future generations. Just because I might not see the fruits of my labor isn't a reason to give up.

The Gift in the Wound

Many people find that their greatest growth and gifts came from having gone through difficult experiences. In his book *The Happiness Hypothesis*, Jonathan Haidt formulates what he calls the "adversity hypothesis," which essentially says that "people need adversity, setbacks, and perhaps even trauma to reach the highest levels of strength, fulfillment and personal development."[5] As discussed in chapter 1, this post-traumatic growth is possible for all of us in our own unique way. Each time we get through something challenging, it has the potential to make us stronger. It can also give us empathy for others who have gone through something similar.

I have a yoga student, Tara, who survived cancer. Prior to her diagnosis she felt lost in life. She hadn't found her passion and struggled with depression and anxiety. She worked in a clothing store and didn't have any close friends. She described just floating through life with no North Star. Getting diagnosed with breast cancer was a terrifying experience, but she shared with me that it was this battle that "woke her up" and ignited her passion for life. When she was cancer-free, she went on to become an oncology nurse and dedicated her life to supporting people with cancer. She is happier than she's ever been and even though she wouldn't wish it on anyone to have such a serious illness, she knows that the experience made her who she is and helped her discover her purpose and joy.

Research on happiness has shown that people who are able to make meaning from their suffering are happier than those who aren't. They don't have to act on it like Tara did; just the awareness can be enough. In one study, people were asked to simply write about a traumatic experience they'd had for an hour. A control group was asked to write about some other, mundane topic. One year later, researchers looked at the medical records of all the participants. They found that the people who wrote about a difficult experience and were able to make meaning out of it through the writing showed significantly fewer health issues than the control group or those who were not able to make meaning out of the event in their writing.[6]

Facing our traumas and difficulties is required if we want to heal. When we deny certain parts of ourselves, our pain only grows. It's like mold that grows fast in the dark and can only be eradicated by exposing it to light. Shining the light of our awareness, empathy, and courage onto the parts of ourselves that we may want to hide is how we can transform our pain into something beautiful.

REFLECTION

What challenging experiences in your life have shaped you? What gifts did you get from these experiences? What gifts can you imagine getting from them?

What We Value and What We Don't

We all have different strengths. Yet when our culture only values certain things as worthy of being celebrated, other qualities get invisibilized, minimized, or even pathologized. For example, we often hear stories of "heroes" who are lauded for their "triumph" over their disabilities by accomplishing things able-bodied people can do, such as amputees running marathons, paraplegic people doing extreme sports, or people like Stephen Hawking writing amazing books on theoretical physics and cosmology despite having

ALS. These are amazing things and should be celebrated. But what about the person who loses their legs and doesn't climb Mount Everest but is able to find their way through their trauma and be self-accepting, patient, and kind? What about the survivor who is debilitated by trauma symptoms but still is able to be a loving parent? What about the person who isn't able to recover from a chronic illness despite their best efforts? What about the person who has to dedicate all their energy to their own self-preservation and has nothing left over to give? Aren't they also worthy of recognition? Aspirational stories can help, and they can harm. Our gifts and strengths are very different from each other; when only certain gifts are celebrated, it creates a pressure to perform (and conform) in ways that are neither everyone's authentic truth nor within their capacity.

My colleague Laura Sharkey is a great example. They work at the nonprofit I cofounded. Laura is autistic and has a chronic illness that causes them intense fatigue (Laura is also nonbinary and uses the pronouns "they" and "them"). Laura is incredibly smart and a great writer, but their illness limits how much they can work and engage. We have crafted a position for them where they work part-time and at the time that their energy levels allow. Laura has put a lot of effort and work into educating us on what it's like for disabled people, especially autistics to survive in the world.[7] They have asked us to reflect on our own work ethic and norms that come from our neurotypical bias. For example, in-person staff meetings can overwhelm autistic people because the way they relate socially can be misinterpreted—many autistic people aren't comfortable making eye contact and their facial expressions can be interpreted as angry or upset. So when Laura has to meet face-to-face, they have to "mask" their autism in order to be relatable. Laura forces themself to smile and make eye contact. But this takes a lot of energy, even for able-bodied autistic people, and with Laura's illness this is especially taxing. For them, written communication is much easier as they can get to the point and not have to jump through the hoops of social norms in order to be heard.

Laura has taught me and our other colleagues a lot. And although on many days I think we just frustrated Laura with our neurotypical bias (it can be hard to break habits we take for granted as being universal for all), I often remind them of the impact they have had because of their willingness to educate us in this way. It is not the obligation of the person who is targeted by discrimination or bias to teach other people about it, and when they do, the feedback may be tough to hear but is a true gift. Because of Laura, our nonprofit is investing in making everything we do more accessible, and it has impacted our curriculum when we train leaders. We still have a lot of work to do, but Laura's willingness to talk with us about their struggles is having a positive ripple effect. Laura can feel frustrated by their lack of energy or ability to "do more" at times. I remind them that they've done a lot and it is up to us able-bodied people with more energy to carry the work forward when Laura can't. Laura's contribution might seem small, but it is significant, and when we can all see our contributions as a collaboration where everyone does what they can, it allows everyone to be celebrated for doing what is realistic and sustainable for them.

Healing versus Cure

Healing looks different for everyone, and healing is not necessarily about being "cured." In his book *Brilliant Imperfection*, Eli Clare, a white, disabled, genderqueer writer and speaker, shares a nuanced and poignant critique of the idea of cure being the end goal for disabled people.[8] He invites readers to hold the ways that disability can be painful, life-limiting, and unwanted without assuming someone is broken, needs fixing, or should be pitied. Our cultural obsession with cure when it comes to disability and other challenges can create harm and marginalization and support a status quo where able-bodied, neurotypical bodies are desirable over all other bodies. Some people's healing does not come through curing what ails them.

I had a client, Sarah, who was one of the most loving and passionate people I'd ever met. She also lived with debilitating trauma from a decade of childhood sexual abuse by a teacher. Thirty years after the experience, she still had daily intrusive thoughts about the perpetrator and suffered from consistent physical and psychological symptoms. She was a brilliant musician and her dream was to share her music with the world. But her trauma constantly got in the way and she would go through periods of intense immobilization and overwhelm that impeded her ability to commit to things for a long time. She came to my yoga classes and for one-on-one somatic work periodically. I never felt that I was able to help Sarah suffer less; rather, I felt like I was accompanying her in her suffering so she felt less alone. I so wanted Sarah to experience some relief for her suffering. I often felt that I was failing her.

At the age of fifty-four, Sarah found out that she had a very rapidly spreading form of cancer. She was admitted to the hospital and soon it became clear she would not make it. She did not want to tell her family she was sick because she had become estranged from her sister and she was overly protective of her mother, who also had health issues. She felt that her sister, Rose, had been conspiring against her even though this was the furthest thing from the truth. A friend eventually shared the news with Sarah's mom and sister, and they flew out immediately to see her at the hospital. They sat by her bedside all day long, and in the last few weeks that Sarah was in the hospital, a tremendous healing occurred. Sarah was able to see that Rose loved her unconditionally. The story that her sister had betrayed and abandoned her completely fell away and Rose became Sarah's lifeline in her last days. In the moments of intense pain and fear, she called for Rose, and Rose was by her side, offering her ice chips and playing her favorite songs and praying with her. Sarah and Rose experienced profound healing even as Sarah was dying of cancer. In those last days of her life, Sarah was able to feel that she was loved and supported. She was able to be held and loved in a way she didn't believe was possible. She died knowing she was not alone. Sarah's healing did not come in the form of a cure but in restoring her faith and connection to her family.

Transforming Trauma

Trauma shapes us. We are shaped by all of our life experiences. Trauma can trap us in the past, it can transform us into something more beautiful and capable than we were before, and everything in between. The process of transformation can be scary, which is why it often seems easier to resist the pull of transformation and stay safely stuck right where we are. Transforming trauma takes courage. The butterfly is a metaphor often invoked when we speak of transformation; the struggle to break out of the chrysalis symbolizing life's struggles and how they help us become stronger. Did you know that before the caterpillar transforms, it first "melts" into a goo? It releases enzymes that literally digest its own body. I love this image because it points to how sometimes transformation can feel like a dissolving of our old self into a new self. The process can feel like death. It's scary!

This is why for so many people it's much easier to hold on to who we are and not let ourselves be changed. This holding on can be the source of our anxiety. Sometimes our anxiety is the energy of fear resisting this pull to transform. By playing it safe, we may feel more in control, but we also miss the chance to risk change and find peace. The way I see it, we have this one precious life. Living a life where we are gripping against change or enduring what is is exhausting. Freedom can't be achieved by denying our past, but it also can't come from being completely defined by it. Freedom comes when we can honor all the parts of ourselves and celebrate the totality of who we are and who we can be.

My friend and colleague Nikki Myers is a yoga teacher, somatic counselor, and addiction/recovery specialist. When she introduces herself to a group in a workshop, she says: "My name is Nikki. I'm an alcoholic, a love addict, a shopping addict, a commercial sex worker, and mother of two living and one deceased child. I'm also a teacher, therapist, leader, activist, mother, grandmother, and great-grandmother." She honors her past and who she is now. She says that all of these are parts of her, and she doesn't want to hide any of them. What would it feel like for you to truly include all the parts of yourself in how you show up in the world?

5

A Few Thoughts about Suffering

How Being with Our Pain Can Open Our Hearts

AS YOU CAN see from the discussion of trauma, suffering comes in many flavors. It can be rooted in personal, interpersonal, or systemic issues. Some suffering is inevitable—things like death, illness, and loss touch everyone in their lifetime. Some of us are protected from certain kinds of suffering, while others face a disproportionate amount of it. In this chapter I'm going to invite you to step back a bit and reflect on your relationship with suffering—your own suffering and the suffering of others. Cultivating a meaningful relationship with suffering is central to working with anxiety. One of the ways we can define anxiety is "a fear of fear." Our fear of facing our suffering can end up making us more anxious than the suffering itself!

Being with Suffering

Being in a conscious relationship with suffering is necessary if we want to be whole and at peace. As Brené Brown says, "Because we have lost our ability to feel pain and discomfort we have transformed it into anger and hate."[1] When this is directed outward, the world feels like our enemy. When this anger is directed inward, we become our own worst enemy. If we want to heal, we have to feel the source of our suffering, not the pain associated with denying it. Lanie's story is a good example of this.

Lanie struggled with an eating disorder her whole life. When she came to me at age fifty, she was still in a cycle of dieting and binging that had begun at age eight. For the first few months of therapy, it was hard for me to get her to talk about anything other than food plans and exercise regimes. She had such a deep hatred of her body, and her whole existence was oriented around her cruel inner voice that constantly told her that she was disgusting. She knew that as a young girl she'd used food to mask her feelings of grief over the death of her father. Her mother and sister had died while Lanie was in her twenties, and this had taken her eating disorder to a new level. Through some deep work in therapy exploring what was beneath the eating disorder, Lanie realized that not only did she use food to numb her grief, but also her grief had been transformed into self-hate, and that fueled her behavior. As painful as it was to struggle with her weight and self-esteem, on some level this was easier than dealing with her grief. Only when she finally let herself feel her grief was she able to find the compassion for herself to feel that she deserved to live and be happy. Her preoccupation with food and her weight was a distraction from the deeper issues that she was avoiding.

REFLECTION

What are your conscious or subconscious beliefs about suffering? What were you taught about suffering in your family of origin? It's okay if your answers seem irrational or unreasonable.

Suffering as Growth

Right now, I am raising a middle schooler. I don't know about you, but middle school was one of the toughest times of my life. I know very few people who have fond memories of sixth grade. It's a tumultuous time socially, hormonally, and academically. Adolescence is when we are faced with the discomfort of these changes in our body and mind. This is our transition from childhood to adulthood, and even when kids have all the support they need, it can feel chaotic and hard. If we weren't faced with trauma prior to adolescence, this can be the first time we face significant suffering. In some ways, how we deal with adolescence can influence how we deal with change and suffering as adults.

Many adolescents tend to blame the outside world for their discomfort. This is a bit of a hallmark of that stage. My sixth-grade son is no exception. He is in a phase of being unhappy with *everything*. Rather than being with his pain, most of the time he is convinced that the world is a horrible place designed by adults to keep him miserable using tactics like homework, video game limits, bedtimes, and vegetables. He is often angry and frustrated, feeling like things never go his way.

In quiet moments together, usually at the end of the day when he's in bed and I come to say goodnight, he'll acknowledge the depths of his pain and admit that it's not caused by anything outside of him. In his case, things are fine, and he wants for nothing. He knows he is privileged and has his basic material needs met as well as loving people around him. He knows his unhappiness cannot be eradicated with unlimited video game time and desserts. When he gets vulnerable in this way, I do my best to listen and simply bear witness to his experience without trying to fix it right away. I try to sit with him in his suffering to show him that he doesn't have to run away from it.

Sometimes I'll offer him tools for how to be with his intense emotions. Things like noticing how the emotion feels in his body and using breath or grounding to not get overwhelmed. I remind him he can write in his journal or reach out to a friend or me or his dad. Sometimes he takes it in, but right now he mostly rolls his eyes and tells me I don't know what I'm talking about. (It takes everything in me not to defensively say to him, "I'm an expert in this stuff! I'm literally writing a book about it!") I know that it took me a lifetime to learn about suffering, and I'm still learning. I spent the first half of my life trying to avoid suffering, and only in the second half of my life am I understanding the wisdom of being with it. I can't make my children avoid what I think is unnecessary anxiety and pain by pushing these ideas onto them. That would be ironic! As much as I'd like that, I know that they'll need to be bumped around by life and learn the lessons in their due time. As parents, being able to be with our children's suffering with patience and compassion (even if what is bothering them seems unreasonable) can be one way we help them navigate the layers of their own pain and help them see that their suffering can be a doorway into deeper self-knowledge and even freedom.

FINDING THE WISDOM IN OUR SUFFERING

Find a comfortable position, take a few moments to get grounded, and connect with your breath. When you're ready, think about your relationship with suffering. Notice how it feels in your body to think about suffering in general, and, if you feel grounded enough, stay with it for a moment. Then imagine that you could turn this feeling into a person, animal, or any type of creature. What does it look like? What does it say to you? What does it want you to know? What does it need from you? Let your imagination flow here as you imagine a dialogue with this wise creature.

Moving Through, Not Around

In *The Book of Joy*, which is a conversation between His Holiness the Dalai Lama and Archbishop Desmond Tutu, the authors write: "Suffering is inevitable . . . but how we respond to that suffering is our choice. Not even oppression or occupation can take away this freedom to choose our response."[2] These wise men feel that we always have a choice, even in the most extreme situations. Both men are known for their compassion and levelheadedness in the face of crisis, and both have a lightness and sense of humor that is unexpected given the atrocities they have experienced and witnessed. In this poignant book, they talk about being with suffering as a doorway to empathy as well as a reminder that we're not alone in our suffering. It is through their acceptance of suffering that they have been able to find hope and even joy.

This is not what we are taught in mainstream Western culture (and many other cultures). Many of us are taught to deny and avoid our pain at any cost. Consumer culture tells us to buy things to make us happy and aspirational marketing has us striving for superficial goals like being thin, wealthy, or popular. We are taught to value appearing happy rather than actually being happy. We often hide our suffering from each other. This perpetuates our isolation and false belief that everyone else is okay and faring better than us. As the saying goes, "What you resist persists." We've got to face our suffering head-on, so that we can transform it, move through it, or be able to be with it without adding to it with our resistance.

Surfing offers an interesting metaphor for this. When I was taking my first surfing lesson on Venice Beach, the instructor explained to me that when I'm paddling out, if a set of waves starts to roll in, I should turn the nose of my board into the waves rather than trying to avoid them. He explained that if I try to avoid the waves they will pummel me to the bottom, but if I meet them with the nose of my board I can surf through them and get to the other side. That all made sense, but when the moment came, my fear had me paddling away from the giant wave coming toward me. I knew in my head I should meet it, but my body automatically had me frantically trying to avoid the powerful force heading my way. Inevitably I'd end up thrown off my board and pushed to the bottom of the sea. I'd come up gasping for air and worried that my board was going to hit me in the head. Finally, after being beaten by the waves many times, I stayed to face the next one. It felt counterintuitive and, although I didn't realize it then, I actually used my resourcing tools of breathing and grounding through my board to be able to not run away. This time, I moved *toward* the wave. And guess what? I went through it! And it flowed over me without much drama. It was quite empowering and made surfing a much more fun activity.

I had another chance to learn this lesson while giving birth to my second son. After laboring for several hours, it came time to push and I hit what is called "transition." This is often the point where people think that maybe they can't push the baby out because it's too hard. For me, transition felt like a hot fire that was going to rip me in half. My midwife was instructing me to push as hard as I could. The pain was so intense, and, to try to manage it, I started visualizing holding my baby and being on the other side of the pain. But each time I did that, the baby would start to move back up the birth canal. You see, I was trying to bypass the pain, and each time I did, I got further away from my goal. Finally, my midwife looked at me very matter-of-factly and said, "I need you to go *here*," and she pointed to the ring of fire. "If you don't, the baby's health could be compromised!" I knew in that moment I needed to do what I teach others to do. I had to move toward the intensity, toward what felt like could be death. On the other side would be my baby in my arms, but I couldn't skip over the process. At that moment, I bore down as hard as I could and pushed right into the pain. It was scary, but I knew there was no choice. A few minutes later Marley was born. I wish I could say that my first thought was about my beautiful baby, but it wasn't; it was, "Thank God that's over!" I was exhausted! Then my body started shaking. I knew it was discharging the trauma of the birth, so I let myself shake and release for a while. Then I was able to feel gratitude for my baby, and for myself for all my hard work!

REFLECTION

What life experiences have you had that have taught you that suffering can be transformed into meaningful growth? What experiences have you had of resisting suffering and inadvertently creating more? What situations or experiences are currently present for you that may be opportunities to stay with discomfort rather than avoiding it?

Suffering and Loss

Middle school, surfing, and childbirth are all examples of difficult situations that are usually ultimately positive. But what about death, loss, and the pain of situations that are tragic and not obviously connected to something generative? Suffering has many flavors, and each type can open us up to something different. The poet Rumi said, "You have to keep breaking your heart until it opens." I love this metaphor because it reminds us that some types of suffering can tenderize our hearts and make us more loving, compassionate, and connected.

My friend and colleague Teo Drake has taught me a lot about suffering, loss, and compassion. Teo is an activist, a practicing

Buddhist, and a yogi. He is also a trans man who has been living with AIDS for the past twenty-five years. In his twenties, he saw many people around him die of AIDS. He saw, firsthand, the terrible way people were treated by the medical community and the culture at large. People with AIDS were treated as if they were disposable because of who they were. And because he was diagnosed before the advent of effective treatment, his diagnosis was considered a death sentence. Not only was he faced with his own illness, every day he saw people in his community dying while also being the targets of hatred and violence. This level of suffering is untenable.

Teo shared a story of going to see the AIDS Memorial Quilt laid out for the last time in its entirety in Washington, DC, one year after his diagnosis. Each rectangle represented someone who had died of AIDS. It stretched out for blocks and blocks, overflowing the entire Washington Mall. Seeing the horror that he had been living made tangible in a piece of art, while being surrounded by thousands of other people there to mourn with him, allowed him to access his grief and feel held in a way he'd never experienced. He shared that "there was a vibrancy in the quilt amidst the horror" and that this is what "vibrancy on the margins looks like." The quilt was a tangible representation of collective suffering; it allowed all who were suffering a way to access their grief more fully together and, in that, for Teo and many others, it offered connection and healing.[3]

Today, Teo's work focuses on supporting those who are most marginalized and discarded by society. You'd think this would make him hard and callous. But the truth is quite the opposite—Teo has an understanding of suffering and loss that allows him to have compassion for the ways that people can be broken down by life. He has been able to extend this compassion beyond his community in a way that I find remarkable (and makes me aspire to do the same). I know that he works hard to do this—to not let the pain he sees daily shut him down. I know that he has been deliberate about letting suffering tenderize his heart rather than make it hard and impenetrable. And I know this is not an easy path to walk. His practices of meditation, contemplation, somatic work, and woodworking are things that support him in approaching suffering in this way. In his case (and for many others in his community) there's no choice. There's no getting away from pain and loss.

Taking in the Suffering of the World

Buddhist philosophy tells us to embrace suffering—not just our own but also the suffering of the world. Engaged Buddhism aims to apply the insights of meditation and dharma teachings to situations of social, political, environmental, and economic suffering and injustice. One of the precepts for practitioners, according to Thich Nhat Hanh, is: "Do not avoid contact with suffering or close your eyes before suffering. Do not lose awareness of the existence of suffering in the life of the world. Find ways to be with those who are suffering, including personal contact, visits, images, and sounds. By such means, awaken yourself and others to the reality of suffering in the world."[4]

Some people are forced to face suffering every day, while others who live in relative comfort may not be. If you fall into the latter group, or in the times in your life when you do, then your work is to consciously choose to stay awake to the suffering of others. If you have the privilege to be able to fall asleep, it's your responsibility to stay awake. For those facing suffering each day, it is also important to use that suffering to open your hearts to others. If our suffering shuts us down and isolates us, it becomes our prison. When we find ways to be with it, it can be our doorway to deeper connection and compassion.

The Buddhist Tonglen meditation, also known as the "taking and sending" meditation, is a practice of breathing in the suffering of others and offering them relief as you breath out. It is a practice of purposely letting your heart open to the suffering of others. This can have the effect of helping us feel less isolated in our own particular type of suffering as well as cultivating compassion for others. Pema Chödrön explains that in doing this, "We become liberated from age-old patterns of selfishness. We begin to feel love for both ourselves and others; we begin to take care of ourselves and others."[5] Thinking about others can help us decrease our suffering. In fact, unhappy people tend to be very focused on themselves and this can fuel their suffering. Letting suffering in can let our hearts open to greater love and gratitude.

TONGLEN MEDITATION

Start by getting grounded and settled. Then, on your in-breath, imagine that you are inhaling heavy, hot air. On your out-breath visualize exhaling cool, light air. Continue with this pattern—breathing in heaviness and breathing out lightness—until it is familiar to you. The heaviness is suffering; the lightness is well-being.

Think about someone you care about who is suffering. Breathe in their suffering; imagine it as heavy, hot air. Let their suffering touch your heart, and then breathe out the cool air of healing and well-being. Repeat this a few times.

Think about your own suffering, and breathe in your own suffering, heavy and hot, and then breathe out the cool air of lightness and healing. Repeat this a few times.

Finally, think about all the others on the planet who might be suffering as you are. Breathe in their suffering with yours, and breathe out the cool air of possibility, healing, and lightness. Repeat this a few times.

A Note about Patience

There's nothing easy about acknowledging and staying with suffering or making meaning of it in time. For some people, life is relentless and when the suffering keeps crashing in on us, it can feel impossible to be with it without being completely torn apart by it. So please don't use the suggestions in this chapter to beat yourself up if life is already beating you up. It's vital that you honor yourself exactly where you are and realize that some people have circumstances that are out of their control that can make it extra hard to be with suffering. Also, doing what I am suggesting can take a lifetime. I am just learning this at age forty-seven and I've dedicated my life to this stuff. As you'll see in the chapters ahead, we cannot face our suffering or that of the world alone.

6

Connection Is the Key

Being Well Requires Us to Depend on One Another

WE CANNOT BE well on our own. In addition to learning how to regulate ourselves and address our trauma and anxiety, we must examine our relationships—both with those we love and in our wider communities. We need each other; accepting this is necessary if we want to truly be well. Cultivating a healthier response to stress—one that moves us toward each other rather than away from each other—must be part of the solution.

We Are Social Animals

> *Throughout our lives we long to love ourselves more deeply and to feel connected to others. Instead, we often contract, fear intimacy, and suffer a bewildering sense of separation. We crave love, and yet we are lonely. Our delusion of being separate from one another, of being apart from all that is around us, gives rise to all of this pain.*
>
> —Sharon Salzberg, from
> *Lovingkindness: The Revolutionary Art of Happiness*[1]

REFLECTION

Take a moment to read the quote above. Notice how it makes you feel. Does it resonate? Does it make you feel defensive? Relieved?

Humans need connection with other people. Not just for our physical survival, as discussed previously, but also for our emotional health and well-being. In fact, a groundbreaking research project in the 1960s proved what many parents already knew intuitively: that our comfort and safety needs are what bond us to each other even more than our physical survival needs. Harry Harlow, a US psychologist, researched rhesus monkeys. If you've taken an introduction to psychology course, you may have come across his work. At that time of his research, the popular thought in the field of psychology was that babies become attached to their mothers because of milk, and milk is what babies need in order to grow into healthy adults. Essentially, the theory was that we attach to other humans because they meet our survival needs. To test this, Harlow separated newborn monkeys from their mothers and put them in a cage with two surrogate mothers.[2] One surrogate was made of wire and dispensed milk, and the other was made of soft cloth but didn't dispense milk. (The cruelty to these innocent animals is not lost on me.)

If the theory that was believed at the time was correct, then the monkeys should have become attached to the wire surrogate because it dispensed milk. That didn't happen. The monkeys attached to the soft surrogate. They spent more time there and only went to the wire surrogate for milk. When they could, they would hold on to the soft surrogate and stretch out to drink from the wire surrogate. These studies suggested that the monkeys bonded to the mother because of physical contact, not feeding needs. In fact, monkeys raised only with the wire, milk-dispensing surrogate were not able to bond with other monkeys once released back into the group, and they showed signs of cognitive impairment. Harlow's studies validated that babies need physical contact in order to thrive, not just milk. His research also showed that when they don't get that contact, it negatively impacts their relationships with other monkeys.

This has interesting implications on human attachment—not just in infancy but also in adulthood. It points to the idea that having safe, secure attachments is vital to our well-being. Bessel van der Kolk says, "Being able to feel safe with other people is probably the single most important aspect of mental health; safe connections are fundamental to meaningful and satisfying lives."[3] Loneliness increases one's risk for premature death. One large public health study found that "lacking social connection carries a risk that is comparable, and in many cases, exceeds that of other well-accepted risk factors, including smoking up to 15 cigarettes per day, obesity, physical inactivity, and air pollution." According to these experts, lack of human connection is at a crisis point.[4]

Connection Is Key

In 2017, former US surgeon general Vivek H. Murthy said that loneliness, which had doubled in the US between 1980 and 1990, has become an epidemic.[5] Even though we are, technically speaking, more able to connect using texts, video chats, and social media, more and more people report feeling isolated and not having relationships that they can count on. Research shows that participation in community events is on a steady decline and that a majority of people, when asked how many close friends they have, said "none." This trend toward greater isolation is having deleterious effects on people and is associated with increased depression and anxiety.[6]

The neuroscience researcher John Cacioppo studied the impact of loneliness on the brain. He found that loneliness is stressful and impacts our immune system and mood. Protracted loneliness can cause people to shut down and shut off from the one thing they need most, which is social interaction. This snowball effect can make loneliness feel like a trap that is impossible to get out of. So when we respond to stress by isolating, it makes things worse.[7]

I know I just spent several chapters giving you tools that require only your individual psyche, nervous system, and body, and these tools are vital. But if I were to stop there, I'd be selling you a big, fat lie. I wish I could breathe and ground myself into well-being. But we cannot be well alone. We need each other. I've heard it said that we have to be healthy and whole and truly love ourselves before someone else can love us. But how can we learn to love ourselves in isolation? We learn love by being in relationship.

When we are struggling, reaching out to ask for help— or even to help someone else—can be a vital part of healing. Connection is key. We must prioritize fostering and maintaining healthy relationships if we are to be well. As a culture, this requires some examination of how we got here so that we can shift the underlying beliefs that have contributed to the increasing isolation that so many are facing. In the first part of this book, I invited you to reflect on your formative life experiences as a source of information for you. In the next part, we'll look at our personal and community connections more deeply, how to build or enhance them, how they impact anxiety, and how this all connects to the wider world. We'll examine ideas and norms that have permeated our culture and that also influence our behaviors and feelings about ourselves. One toxic idea is the idea that we should be fine alone.

The Myth of Rugged Individualism

I've already discussed how the idea of rugged individualism—the myth that all individuals can succeed on their own and thus be happy—impacts our understanding of systemic trauma. This concept has also permeated the mental health, healing, and self-help fields, which, in an attempt to empower us to not feel like victims to what we think we can't control, can inadvertently put undue blame and stress on us. There is often an implication that we should be able to heal on our own through hard work and perseverance. There are certainly individual things we can do to feel good, but it's unfair and untrue to imply that we can be okay in isolation. We need other people in order to be happy and healthy. It doesn't make us needy or codependent. It doesn't make us weak. It makes us human.

Part of being healthy and whole is our ability to be in relationships that are mutual and supportive. Embracing our vulnerability as a courageous act, as Brené Brown is so famous for saying, means that we admit that we need each other and don't hide behind a veneer of being okay in isolation. I wrote my college entrance essay on the idea that, ultimately, we are alone—we are born alone, and we die alone. I remember when my father read it, he teared up. It broke his heart that I felt this way. I, on the other hand, found it empowering. Embracing this belief absolved me of the need to be vulnerable and open to others. It made me feel in control. That served me, to some extent, but ultimately it became a defense I had to release. So many people can get caught in this isolation trap. Some people have the financial ability to pay people for services rather than lean into their relationships for support. This "convenience" can also fuel alienation and isolation.

I had a client, Sue, who was a high-powered CEO of a bank. She and her parents and two younger sisters moved to the US from China when she was six. Her father was a savvy business man, and their family had a fairly good life in the US until her father abandoned the family when Sue was twelve. Her mother did not have any formal education or any way to support her children, so she had no choice but to take jobs cleaning houses to make ends meet. The girls saw how much their mother struggled, and as the oldest, Sue stepped in to help with her sisters while her mother worked. Sue vowed never to be in that position, and she built her whole life with the goal of never depending on anyone to take care of her. She excelled in school and dedicated all her energy to her career. She had a well-paying corporate job, a beautiful house, a nice car, and a lot of money in her savings account. She took care of her younger sisters financially when they needed it, and the closest relationships she had outside of her sisters were with her personal assistant and her two pugs. She worried about money all the time and never felt secure. She really wanted a partner and children of her own, but none of her relationships lasted more than a few months.

Sue first came to me after her fortieth birthday. She was frustrated because she was able to accomplish everything she wanted in her career using her will and smarts. She thought that finding a partner should be the same—she was on all the dating sites and she even paid a matchmaker to help set her up with quality men. By the time Sue came to me, she was at her wits' end. Her plan to have two children of her own was being seriously threatened. She was considering getting pregnant by any guy just to have kids, figuring she could break up with him and raise the children on her own. What stood out to me about Sue was that she would never admit that she wanted connection. Her plan to have children felt like another thing on her to-do list, not a heartfelt desire.

Sue was so disconnected from her own vulnerability that I had a very hard time connecting with her. As her therapist, I felt like one of her employees. She would pay me to just listen to her. She would come into her session, dump all her thoughts onto me, and leave. Most of my attempts to slow her down and have her connect to her deeper feelings were ignored. The only feelings she could tolerate were frustration and irritation. She was very resistant to being vulnerable in front of me. Finally, after over a year of therapy (and some gentle coaxing from me), she started to allow herself to connect to her vulnerability. She began to tap into feelings of sadness and grief around her father and the predicament he left her family in. She was terrified of these feelings, but she came to see that only by integrating these feelings and finding compassion for that scared little girl could she be available for a truly connected relationship.

You see, the little girl in Sue was committed to never being rejected again, so to be in a relationship where there was any risk was simply not an option. This is a catch-22, of course. When we avoid the pain something might cause us, we end up avoiding the source of our potential happiness and satisfaction as well. Relationships are always a risk; resilience means entering into them knowing that we can survive if things don't work out. When we refuse to feel vulnerable feelings, we live a life of avoidance—avoiding potential pain and rejection, avoiding difficult feelings, avoiding ourselves. We can experience a lot of growth in relationships because they make us confront parts of ourselves we can avoid when we're alone.

I made a declaration similar to Sue's as a child. I saw how disempowered my mother was in her marriage, and I swore I would be an empowered woman who never depended on a man for anything. So much of my work in my own marriage has been about opening myself up and letting myself need my husband. The first time Paul had to go away for a few months for a work trip, I found myself distancing from him in the weeks prior to his departure. When he asked me why I had become distant (I hadn't been conscious of any of this), I realized that in order to not feel my sadness about him leaving, I was shutting down. It's like part of me was wanting to show myself that I didn't need him anyway, so who cares if he leaves! I tend to be so damn self-sufficient that I can make it hard for Paul to do anything for me. (He has explicitly told me this, by the way). Then it becomes a self-fulfilling prophecy that I need to do everything on my own. I'm learning more and more that I need to make space for others to support me; I can't block them with my inflated sense of independence and self-sufficiency. It's scary because I risk being disappointed or rejected, but the alternative keeps me trapped in my safe bubble all alone not needing anyone.

I had to do the same thing in my friendships. Until my mid-twenties, most of my friendships were with people who needed me so much that I never worried they would leave me. It was draining, and I often felt lonely even when I had people around me. Through a lot of personal work in therapy and doing my own self-reflection on my tendency to be drawn to people who needed me, I started to change this pattern. I slowly dared to engage in friendships with strong, integrated people who I could lean on and who could lean on me. It was scary but necessary work.

One of my best friends now, Tessa Hicks Peterson, taught me about this balance. I met her in a Brazilian martial arts class when I first moved to Los Angeles. She was an amazing athlete who exuded confidence and kindness. I really liked her but found her intimidating as well. We started becoming friends, and one day she spontaneously showed up at my house in tears, snot dripping down her face, sharing that she had just broken up with her boyfriend. She sat on my couch sobbing, telling me how hard it was and how sad she was even though she knew it was for the best. I remember thinking, "Wow, she is so confident and strong and she's not afraid of being so sad in front of me." I didn't think I had ever let myself sob like that in front of someone else. When I separated from my first husband the year before, I only cried about it in private. To others, I would explain why it was the best thing for us, and that I was fine. The thing is, I *was* fine. And I also could have let myself be sad in front of my friends. I just didn't trust that they'd know what to do and I didn't want to burden them. I was so used to taking care of others that I didn't really know how to let others take care of me. My current friendships are mutual and reciprocal. I'm able to ask for support when I need it, and I'm able to give support when my friends need it. I understand now that needing someone doesn't make me needy. It's healthy!

The concept of being "needy" refers more to when we don't have a secure sense of self, and we rely solely on others to define us or validate us. This can be disempowering and anxiety producing, and it can put us at risk of being taken advantage of. Yet when we refuse to rely on others, we lose a part of humanity that is rooted in our connectivity. Relationships based on reciprocity can allow us to feel needed and supported; they remind us of our connection to all things in a way that can bring depth and meaning to life. Feeling connected in a healthy and empowered way helps us feel secure and reduces feelings of anxiety or overwhelm.

The Limits of Individual Well-Being

Jack Kornfield, a prominent Buddhist teacher, interviewed Buddhist practitioners who had experienced ecstatic states of awakening, grace, and oneness with the Divine through years of study, dedicated spiritual practice, and monastic life away from regular society. He found that after these experiences, when it came time to return home and face life's struggles, many felt unprepared. What they had experienced in their personal meditation and self-reflection processes did not necessarily translate into their daily, relational lives. In fact, Kornfield says, often the real work begins once we reenter life, whether we've been on a retreat or doing our personal work away from others in another way. "We all know that after the honeymoon comes the marriage, after the election comes the hard task of governance. In spiritual life it is the same: After the ecstasy comes the laundry."[8]

I had a client, Jeff, who came to me because he couldn't figure out why he wasn't happy. He had achieved his goal of owning his own company and making a lot of money by age forty. He was healthy, traveled the world, could work part-time, and basically had the freedom to do whatever he wanted. He said to me, "I spent my life climbing this mountain, and now that I'm at the top, it's lonely." He had put all his energy into individualistic goals and had failed to build strong relationships and community. None of his so-called success mattered because he was lonely. What he truly longed for was community and connection, but he had sacrificed that to chase material success.

Just like Jeff (and Sue), we can get stuck in a fruitless search for happiness pursuing individualistic means, but all the therapy, exercise, money, and health in the world can't make us truly happy. At least not in a complete way. Today some people can build an entire life that is devoid of meaningful relationships. Modern life has made it easier and easier to isolate ourselves. Our ancestors needed each other to survive—we needed help building homes; tending to children, animals, and gardens; protecting each other. It is actually part of our biology to feel bad when we're alone because, for our ancestors, it meant our chances for survival were compromised. Today many of us can sit in our homes, have almost anything we need delivered to us, and never speak to or see an actual human being. Many of our lives run at a level of convenience that limits the necessity for human interaction. This can perpetuate the myth of individualism both because it isolates us and because it disconnects us from the web of life and our participation in it. Suddenly it can feel like we are passive observers of life rather than active participants in it.

In some ways, isolation due to convenience is an affliction impacting more affluent communities. They can afford to pay for the conveniences that contribute to a weak relational support system. (Poor and working-class people often have no choice but to rely on each other as they cannot afford to hire help or order what they want online.) There are also many people who are isolated not by choice—older people are especially at risk, as well as people with disabilities and mental health conditions, people who have had to leave their family and community to find work, and others. Ultimately loneliness does not discriminate; it just might come in slightly different flavors for different people.

In some communities, especially under-resourced ones dealing with poverty, drugs, and over-policing, people can feel a loss of agency and self-determination in the face of the obstacles they face daily. In these communities there are also beautiful examples of the ways people take care of each other and create ways to have some self-determination despite their external challenges.

Community centers, churches, and affinity groups are some examples. The investor and venture capitalist Arlan Hamilton, a queer, Black woman, started Backstage Capital, a seed-stage investment fund that invests in start-ups run by underrepresented founders who are typically overlooked by mainstream funders. She reminds us that "underrepresented doesn't mean people who are down and out; they're people who have done more with less." In these communities, where separation is not really an option, sticking together during crisis is an act of social and political resistance against a world not oriented toward their care.

Addiction

As discussed previously, addiction is often rooted in an inability to cope with trauma, anxiety, or depression. It's also often seen as an individual problem that needs to be addressed by the person getting sober. But connection is key to healing here, too. Johann Hari, the author of Lost Connections, says that "the opposite of addiction is not sobriety; the opposite of addiction is connection."[9] Unfortunately, our culture's approach to addiction has long been to criminalize those with addictions and treat them as if they have an individual problem that can be solved in isolation. Loved ones are encouraged to shut someone out if they are using—this "tough love" approach is hailed as necessary in not enabling the behavior. People with resources typically go to treatment facilities; people without resources go to jail. In general, our culture deals with people with addiction by separating them from society, loved ones, and resources while shaming their behavior. Based on new research on addiction, stress, and isolation, this is the opposite of what people with addiction need. Yet it has been common practice and continues to be in the US and other Westernized cultures, although others are leading the way to finding better approaches. For example, in 2001 Portugal decriminalized drugs. Instead of being arrested, users are now offered support and counseling. The country has had a staggering drop in problematic drug use.[10]

Bruce Alexander is a psychologist and addiction researcher. He's known for his "rat park" study.[11] In this study, he found that when rats were in isolation, they would consume large amounts of morphine when it was made available to them—often to the point of death. But when the rats were housed in what he called "rat park"—an ecosystem where they were with other rats and had places to play and sleep—they showed a decreased preference for the morphine. Alexander says that we need to talk more about "social recovery," not individual recovery, when it comes to addiction. Addiction is often rooted in an inability to tolerate what we are feeling—things are overwhelming and we feel we have no choice but to numb out to escape. Breaking addictive behaviors requires us to find ways to be present with ourselves, and this takes support from others.

Transforming the Stress Response

In chapter 1 I spoke in depth about the fight-or-flight response as a typical response to stress or a perceived threat. I also mentioned another response that has only more recently been studied—the "tend-and-befriend" response. Tending refers to nurturing and protective behaviors, and befriending has to do with building social networks that can offer protection and safety. Research shows that this latter response can decrease our stress and increase our hope. It can actually help relieve our anxiety.

Kelly McGonigal devotes an entire chapter in her book *The Upside of Stress* to the idea that caring creates resilience.[12] When we are able to respond to stress by tending and befriending, it reduces our fear. She lifts up research that has proven that caring for others triggers the biology of courage and creates hope. One interesting study at UCLA showed that when people are invited to squeeze a stress ball in response to seeing a friend receive a painful shock, their brains remain in a state of fear, but when they are invited to hold the hand of the person receiving the shock, activity increases in the reward and caregiving regions of the brain and their fear response decreases.[13] This points to the idea that shutting ourselves off from the suffering of others keeps us stuck in fear. When we extend our care and connect, we can find hope and even ease amidst suffering.

McGonigal also explains how research shows that responding to trauma by helping others allows people to be happier and find more meaning in life. This has been called "altruism born of suffering" by psychology professor Ervin Staub. He studies Holocaust survivors and their behavior during their imprison-ment. Survivors who reported helping others in some way showed increased altruism. Staub found this to be true in the aftermath of other mass traumas as well. He found a correlation between how much someone suffered and how much they helped. Increased suf-fering also increased helping behavior.[14] This goes counter to the fight-or-flight theory. Or perhaps we can see it as being consistent with the animal response to discharge traumatic stress. Banding together to help after a traumatic event can be seen as a form of discharge where we're able to use the energy that was mobilized to deal with an inescapable circumstance to help others. In fact, this makes sense on a biological level: after overwhelming events, connecting with others is a very natural way to feel like there's something you can do. Retreating or separating can sometimes makes things worse and keep the energy bottled up inside of us.

From Fight-or-Flight to Tend-and-Befriend

Although there are many instances of people reaching out to help one other in situations of stress and trauma, these days it can seem like conflict and division are the norm rather than connection and care. This is partly a result of a media that thrives on reporting sensationalist, negative events that inspire fear in us. Media outlets are vying for our attention, so the simpler a story is, and the more it catches our eye, the more likely people are to read it. I actually believe that the world is a much kinder place than we see in the news. But those stories don't grab our attention. How often do we read headlines that highlight people supporting each other? Unless it's a supremely heroic act, those everyday acts of kindness largely go unnoticed in the news. This is why we need to see them around us in our lived experience. If we look for them, we are likely to find them, even in the most unsuspecting of circumstances.

Tend-and-befriend is just as much a part of our human nature as fight-or-flight. We are wired for connection and collective care, and when we lean into that part of our nature, we trigger courage and hope—on a biological level! Yet mainstream culture has promoted an individualistic focus on responding to stress by fighting or running away. I believe this may be one of the core issues causing our suffering—not just personally but socially and even globally. One question we can ask ourselves is how can we cultivate a healthier response to stress and anxiety? We've looked at things we can do on an individual level; now let's look at what we can do in our relationships and communities.

Being well is about coming back into right relationship with ourselves, each other, and the planet. It is about remembering our interdependence with all things. We are part of this amazing web of life; when we are not reminded of this consistently, it wears away at our life force and spirit.

Indigenous Wisdom

I want to make it clear that the ideas I'm sharing—especially those around connection—are not new. Other cultures have historically centered interdependence and right relationship in their worldviews. Because I live on land that was stolen from the Indigenous peoples who lived here, it feels important to honor that, although not all Native American nations are the same, in many, connection and right relationship are viewed as the foundation for peace and happiness. This includes relationships with other people, ancestors, nature, and Spirit. Indigenous wisdom is thousands of years old and also lives on today in all those Native Americans who have survived colonization and work to preserve their traditional ways of life. For example, the Lakota saying *Aho Mitakuye Oyasin* means "all my relations," and is a daily mantra said by Lakota people to remind them of what is the most important thing—to live in right relationship with all parts of life.[15]

If part of your anxiety is tied to being isolated or disconnected, imagine how you might prioritize building supportive relationships by reaching out when you are afraid rather than shutting down. Nurturing our tend-and-befriend response and building what I like to call our "connection ecosystem" is a key to individual and collective healing and well-being.

7

Creating a Connection Ecosystem

Building Resilience in Community

THIS CHAPTER IS an invitation to reflect on what I like to call our "connection ecosystem" so that we can consider the places in our lives where we can foster more meaningful relationships of all kinds. Cultivating "biodiversity" in our relational life can be one way to buffer ourselves from the negative impact of anxiety and find more meaning and inspiration in our lives. By biodiversity, I mean all the different ways that we interact with and engage with other people. Deep, enduring friendships are certainly important, but caring for humanity (and feeling cared for) contributes to our sense of happiness and wholeness. It is also part of contributing to a kinder, more just world. We need to widen our circle of compassion, and we do this by extending our attention and care beyond our immediate circle of people we're familiar with.

When we think of connection and relationships as a biodiverse ecosystem, we can begin to appreciate all the different ways that connection and care can happen—some of our relationships are complex, enduring, and intimate, such as with a partner, family member, friend, or even coworkers. I call these *core relationships.* Others can be fleeting or surface-level, such as with someone next to us on the bus, workers at stores we frequent, or a neighbor. I call these *community connections*. There are also the people and communities that we may never encounter but we have invisible connections to—these can range from the workers who picked our food to the politicians making decisions that impact us. And, of course, there's our relationship with ourselves.

When we consider all these dynamics, we can see a whole ecosystem of relationships that can either bolster our sense of wholeness, well-being, and peace or undermine it. We need this ecosystem to be strong in order to be well. Just like in nature, where there is a symbiotic relationship between the soil, microorganisms, bugs, plants, and animals, only when humans are in a symbiotic relationship with each other (and nature) can we truly be well.

Consider the person who has two or three highly supportive and caring friends that they will do anything for, as well as a tight-knit family, but they are rude to servers at restaurants, yell at slow-moving drivers in front of them, or don't tip people in service jobs or show them gratitude and respect. There is a disconnect there that, even if they are not aware of it, keeps that person from being totally integrated and whole. That person's work is to take the time and energy to acknowledge the humanity of all those around them, even if they believe they have nothing in common. You see, when we only value certain people, and others are disposable or invisible to us, we subconsciously perpetuate the fragmentation and disconnection in the world and inside ourselves.

What about the person who knows everyone in their neighborhood by name, chats up the mailperson and janitor, and is a great worker at their job, but has no close friends to support them and spends most of their time outside of work alone, not by choice? This too is not a healthy balance.

REFLECTION

Take a moment to reflect on your connection ecosystem. Are there places where you feel a sense of warmth and authentic relationship? If so, where? Where is this connection lacking? Write your answer or draw a picture to symbolize your connection ecosystem.

Connection as Survival

There is an interesting video of an experiment called the "still face experiment."[1] It is an interaction between a mother and her one-year old child. In the first part of the experiment, the mother is very responsive to her baby. When the baby laughs, the mother laughs back; when the baby points, the mother looks to see what she is pointing at; and when the baby reaches her hands out, the mother responds by holding her hands. It's clearly an exchange where both are reacting to each other with delight. In the second part of the experiment, the mother is told to just keep a still face. She looks at her child with a neutral expression and, this time, when the baby makes sounds or points, the mother doesn't do anything. She remains still and with a neutral expression on her face. We see the child try several things to get the mother to respond— she laughs, points again, and claps her hands. After about forty-five seconds the baby screeches, and after about ninety seconds she starts to get visibly distressed and upset, crying and looking away. When the mother begins to engage again, the baby calms down and is happy and playful again.

This need to feel seen and responded to never goes away. We are hardwired for connection, and when we don't have it, it is very stressful. It literally creates a sympathetic response in our nervous system as if we are in danger. We may not screech and cry like the baby in the still face experiment, but the stress of disconnection can be at the root of much of our anxiety and pain. For some of us, this is the missing piece. We can do all the personal work in the world, but without meaningful relationships, life will feel empty and we will never feel truly secure.

At the heart of this book is the idea that we cannot truly heal in isolation. Harville Hendrix, author of the best-selling book *Getting the Love You Want*, says that it is the relationship that heals the individual, not the reverse.[2] Sometimes we can learn to love ourselves by learning to love someone else in an authentic and healthy way and by being able to trust enough to receive love and support. Relationships touch parts of ourselves we can avoid when we are alone. Relationships help us confront the parts of ourselves that need love the most. This can be true in all kinds of relationships, but is especially true in core relationships.

Core Relationships

Core relationships can refer to intimate partners, friends, family members, or work colleagues. These are relationships that are not fleeting, and that require us to do ongoing work to maintain them and keep them healthy. Some of these relationships are chosen (such as friends or partners) and others are not (such as family or work colleagues).

In these relationships, feeling disconnected can create conflict, tension, resentment, and isolation. If we treat the symptoms, it can feel like an uphill battle, but if we nourish the roots of connection, many of the symptoms fall away and the deeper issues can be addressed with more ease. If a flower is dry and withering because it needs water, and the soil is depleted, dripping water on the leaves or cutting off the dry parts doesn't fix the problem.

You can do whatever you like to the flower, but until you tend to the soil and the roots, it can't flourish. Relationships are the same way. If disconnection is the disease, superficial approaches that address only the symptoms of disconnection won't work. We need to start by admitting that what we want is connection, then real healing can begin.

Connection can mean different things to different people. For me it's a feeling of being on the same team, so to speak. It's a feeling of warmth and safety and giving each other the benefit of the doubt. When I am connected to someone, I am not concerned about conflict; I know that should it arise, we can work through it with kindness and mutual respect. When I am connected to someone I see their humanity and that they are doing their best. If they let me down, I don't take it personally.

REFLECTION

What does connection mean to you? What does it feel like?

Nurturing connection is something I try to make a priority in my marriage. Two working people raising children can be a natural setup for disconnection and the anxiety that can get triggered by that. When we don't make time to nurture our relationship, frustration and resentment inevitably begin to fester. I'll start to focus on how Paul doesn't do enough housework or needs to take better care of himself. He will get irritated by me and tell me that I am always complaining and micromanaging him. On the surface it can look like we are irritated and disagreeing, but beneath the surface is usually a longing to feel closer. When I'm not aware of this, I might sit Paul down and tell him I need him to help me around the house more, or that I'm concerned for his health since I'm noticing he's missing his morning walks. I'll have a list of things ready to prove my point in case he resists. He might tell me that I'm pushy and that he feels like I'm always criticizing him. Those conversations, even when we try our hardest to communicate consciously, are usually tense, and we both walk away feeling bad. He feels criticized and I feel resentful. Because we're not addressing our disconnection, the conversation is inevitably polarizing and makes us feel further away from each other.

Many couples get into this gridlock where disconnection fuels our anxiety and makes it harder to reconnect. When we feel rejected or abandoned, it can be very hard to reach out and admit what we truly want. We might lash out or shut down instead. When we can be with our desire to feel more connected without defending against it (hint: you can use the somatic resourcing tools to do this), it can allow us to reach out differently. When I'm able to do this, instead of sitting Paul down to share my list of complaints, I'll come to him and ask if he wants to hang out or go for a walk. I'll let him know I miss him and want to feel closer to him. It helps him when I can be clear about what that looks like. For me, it means spending two or three evenings a week together instead of disappearing into our own worlds after the kids go to bed. It also means having a date night at least twice a month. He doesn't need as much one-on-one time to feel connected, but he understands that I do. Knowing what our loved ones need in order to feel connected, and then finding a compromise, is important. The point is, if we come from a place of admitting that what we truly want is connection, it can pave the way toward a smoother resolution when conflict arises.

This can be especially true with our children. Parents can get caught up in all the things we want our kids to do to be healthy, happy, and good people—things like doing well in school, eating healthy foods, having a balanced use of technology, getting enough sleep, developing good habits of hygiene and cleanliness, being helpful around the house, treating others with respect, and so forth. When I focus too much on all the things I want my kids to do without nurturing a feeling of connection, they start to feel like all I do is bark orders at them and they shut down. I start to feel resentful ("If you just did what I said, I wouldn't have to keep telling you what to do!"), and I don't feel the warmth for them that I'd like to. This can make me feel like parenting is simply being a cook, maid, and referee. That's a terrible feeling, because what I crave is warmth and connection with my kids, and I know it's what they ultimately need from me as well. I don't want to be like the metal surrogate mother in Harry Harlow's research, giving them what they need without the warmth that is vital to their well-being.

I'm working on letting at least half of my interactions with my children not be about telling them what to do. This is really hard and I'm not entirely able to pull it off yet, to be honest. This might look like wading through the piles of laundry and food wrappers in my twelve-year old's room to just sit with him and chat about his day or tell him I love him. It takes everything for me to not give him a speech about cleanliness and responsibility, but I know that conversation will only shut him down. A five-minute check-in about how he's doing and what he wants for dinner helps to build a reserve of connection so that later I can gently say to him, "Hey, pick the stuff up off your floor, okay?" When I take time to simply be with him—this can mean watching a TV show together, or bantering about a silly topic—it makes the other stuff easier. Relationships need a reserve of connected feelings in order to face the difficult stuff. Little things can go a long way.

This goes for friendships as well. Different things can get in the way of having truly connected friendships. Communication is key in all kinds of relationships, and many people find that lack of communication can fuel a sense of disconnection that prevents friendships from having the depth and meaning that is possible. Technology can help us stay connected, but it can also get in the way, especially in friendships where personal interaction is not a given. In the last few years, I've gotten in the habit of texting my friends rather than calling them. I also get to see updates from many of them on social media, which can make me think I'm connected to them. But am I? I've noticed that even if I've "communicated" with multiple friends in one day via text or social media, that feeling of connection is fleeting. I can still feel lonely and disconnected a few minutes after the interaction. Yet when I call and have an actual conversation or, even better, when I video call them or see them in person, it's drastically different. The feeling of warmth and connection is enduring. It fills me in a way that digital interactions can't.

Fostering connection in our friendships requires more than just communicating offline—it requires us to trust, be vulnerable, set appropriate boundaries, and ask for what we need. It also requires us to tolerate disappointments (appropriately), accept people where they are, and get good at having difficult conversations. When we prioritize connection, this can set the stage for all of this.

REFLECTION

In your close relationships, how do you know when you need more connection? What thoughts, feelings, or behaviors do you exhibit? What does it feel like in your body?

TOLERATING DISCONNECTION PRACTICE

Imagine a relationship where there is tension that may be due to feeling disconnected. As you imagine this person, notice what you feel in your body: sensations, emotions, impulses, or images. Sit with whatever comes up. Remember to use your somatic resources. As you stay with what emerges, notice what else comes up. Are there other emotions or memories present?

As you feel the disconnection, can you imagine also what it might feel like to reach out to that person rather than separate? What might that look like or sound like?

In difficult times, you might ask yourself, "Do I want to be right or do I want to be connected?" This doesn't mean we sacrifice our truth for connection; it might mean we front-load connection in order to get to the truth. There are certainly situations where giving people the benefit of the doubt is not appropriate. If a person has been physically or emotionally abusive to you, setting strong boundaries and taking space (or leaving the situation altogether) may be the best thing you can do. If your emotional or physical safety is at risk, it's not appropriate to connect before you've had certain boundaries respected.

Gratitude is an amazing connector. A friend shared with me that she and her wife were caught in a similar gridlock to what I described earlier with my husband. They decided to go to couples therapy. The therapist suggested that they start expressing more gratitude to each other. My friend thought the suggestion was silly and superficial. She wanted to talk about their problems and how to deal with them. She didn't feel that she could express gratitude authentically if they hadn't addressed their issues first. When I had dinner with my friend a few months later, she shared that the tension with her wife had pretty much cleared up. Her wife started sending her short texts during the day expressing her gratitude for her—things like, "I'm really grateful that you're such a loving mom to our daughter" or "Thank you for always preparing such a yummy dinner on the nights I have to work late." This actually made my friend feel good, and when her wife would come home from work, she found herself less inclined to be critical. Over time, their negativity dissipated and they both felt more warmth for each other. They were able to sit down and have some difficult conversations about their relationship without getting defensive. The small gestures of gratitude filled their well enough to be able to face the challenges with more ease.

We can think about this from a physiological perspective. When we don't feel connected to someone, our nervous system can go into a sympathetic response (activation). We may be in a state of fight-or-flight or shutdown. When we connect, even if it's just through a hug, some eye contact, or an expression of gratitude, it can trigger a feeling of settling and even safety. Research has shown that when we hug someone we care about for just six seconds, our brain produces oxytocin, which gives us a feeling of warmth and security. From this feeling of connection and safety, communication is much more effective. In other words, we trigger the tend-and-befriend response discussed earlier.

GRATITUDE COMMUNICATION PRACTICE

Next time you feel tension with a partner, friend, or loved one, before you express yourself try these steps: (1) take a deep breath and get grounded before you speak, (2) tell the person one thing you are grateful for about them, and (3) share your concern, thought, or request.

Seeking out and strengthening at least a few healthy friendships where we feel safe and seen can also buffer us against life's external stressors. When we have places where we can let our guard down and trust another person, it can fill our well so that we can face difficulty with more internal resilience. And knowing there are people we can turn to when we feel beaten down can give us the wherewithal to persevere in the face of disappointment or pain.

Fostering Connection at Work

Professional relationships need to be grounded in connection as well. I see this come up with the executive director of my nonprofit, Anita Akhavan. We work closely together on many projects year-round. We both pride ourselves on being efficient, and we're also friends outside of work. Last month my workload outside the nonprofit peaked. I was stressed. I wasn't responding to Anita's emails at my regular pace, and she got frustrated. Our email communication became strained, and I started to feel pressured by her to get stuff done at a pace that wasn't possible for me at that moment. She sent me one message indicating that I had committed to get something done by a certain date and now we were past the date. I sent her a snarky response implying that if I were getting paid for this work I wouldn't have had to take on an extra job that month to cover my bills. Needless to say, it was getting tense.

Finally, I invited Anita over for a cup of tea. I shared with her what was going on for me and that I was feeling maxed out. I apologized for being behind. She then shared with me that she had just gone through a breakup so she was feeling particularly sensitive to not being responded to. As soon as we each knew what was going on for the other person, all the tension went away. What was happening beneath our snarky email exchanges was a desire for the other person to realize that we were struggling. We now have a policy with each other that when we need the other to know what's going on for us, we just ask. We don't need to spend a lot of time on our personal stuff during work hours, but we can at least name the things that might be getting in the way of smooth communication.

Some research points to lack of connection in the workplace as a major culprit for loneliness and the anxiety or depression that can result from it.[3] People who spend eight to ten hours a day at work without feeling connected to their coworkers can feel isolated even though they are around people all day. I've spent several years working with the staff at various organizations offering trainings on collaboration, self-care, and communication. I usually get called in when there is conflict, gossip, and lack of cohesion amongst the team. When I first started doing this, I would come in with a PowerPoint presentation containing all the information they needed on the impact of stress, stress management tools, and communication strategies. People appreciated the information, but something was missing. I would often leave the workshops feeling incomplete.

As I began to understand the need for interpersonal connection more, I began starting off the workshops by giving people the opportunity to relate with each other. I usually have them get into small groups to talk about what brings them to this work. Sometimes we just do silly exercises that get everyone laughing together. When people had more time to connect with each other, even on a superficial level, they began to light up. They were able to take in the information I offered more fully and use the tools with each other more easily. The feedback I started getting was that the best part of the workshops was the part where participants got to know each other better.

When people feel more connected to each other, work can feel more inspiring and communication is naturally better. They also support each other to practice self-care and ask for help when they need it. I can teach all the communication tools in the world, but if folks aren't fostering connection, saying the right words isn't enough. I see it in my own staff at my nonprofit.

Whenever we make the time in a staff meeting to check in and see how everyone is doing, spirits are high and collaboration is smoother. When we get overly focused on our to-do lists without taking time to check in, the work is clunky and slower and people are more likely to trigger each other or have miscommunications.

So many organizations experience staff challenges that are rooted in not feeling heard or seen. This raises anxiety and creates an atmosphere of defensiveness or apathy. Some of the solutions are fairly simple—for example, ask people how they are doing. Do it with sincerity, like you actually want to know. Make time in meetings to do check-ins. Create opportunities for people to connect personally in trainings and continuing education. If people are working remotely, you can use video chats and breakout groups to foster more personalized connection and communication. Don't work through your lunch hour; use it as a chance to sit together and talk about nonwork topics. It can feel difficult if people already feel behind and like there's too much on their plates, but fostering connection is like filling your tank with gas: it gives people the motivation and wherewithal to do their work more effectively and even joyfully. If you are in a position of authority at your workplace, use that power to encourage an atmosphere that is supportive of these relationships and see for yourself how people become more inclined to work with each other and get stuff done. It's important to not use this idea to put all the blame on staff if they are unhappy. Often there are very real structural issues that impact staff well-being, such as being underpaid, being asked to work too many hours, and lack of authentic responsiveness and support from upper-level management. Checking in with people is one thing, but making change as a result of what is heard is also vital. The anxiety of disconnection is real, and so is the anxiety of unrealistic expectations and lack of support.

BUILDING CONNECTION AT WORK REFLECTION

If you feel disconnected from the people you work with, what can you do to foster connection?

Connection and Power

It's important to note that power dynamics influence relationships substantially. When we don't acknowledge the role of power in our relationships, there can be an unfair burden placed on people with less power and, conversely, not enough responsibility placed on those with more power. When my staff are feeling unhappy with certain things at work, I need to understand that they may feel afraid to speak up because they perceive their job to be on the line. I might fancy myself the most fair and kind person in the world, so I think they have nothing to worry about. But, truth be told, I do have the power to fire someone or change their role. As Spider-Man's Uncle Ben said, "with great power comes great responsibility." When I have the power, it is my responsibility to attend to the well-being of my staff and do my best to create an atmosphere where they feel they can express themselves.

Some relationships have clear power dynamics, such as those between supervisors and supervisees, teachers and students, parents and children, and doctors and patients. If you find yourself in the power position in any of these dyads, consider the different role and power you have to support a connected and authentic dynamic. Some relationships also carry historical or systemic power dynamics, such as those between women and men, people of color and white people, and wealthy and poor people. This can add a layer of complexity. Systemic power inequalities run through our everyday lives, and their long histories can often intensify the dynamic. Take a situation where a Black woman is the boss and a white man is her subordinate. There are some settings, especially male-dominated and/or majority-white ones, where she may feel unable to assert herself with her supervisee, even if, technically speaking, she has the power.

Take a moment to reflect on the way that power, both role-based and identity-based, could be influencing some of your relationships. Reflecting on these dynamics may reveal to you some pain points in these relationships. I have several female friends who work in finance. Two of them are in senior positions, yet they shared with me that they constantly confront assumptions from men about their capacity to do their job because of their gender. It is a constant stressor and something they manage in all of their professional interactions. One of the women is Latina, and she finds herself also navigating a similar dynamic with white women. These patterns make their jobs exponentially more stressful than those of their white, male colleagues.

One thing to consider is that often the person with power is less aware of the impact of their power on their relationships. One small example from my life came when I needed to hire a babysitter to help me with my kids. At first, I expected that she would tell me her rate and I would pay said rate. Sometimes she watched one of my kids and sometimes both. Some days I needed her to make meals and others not. I realized that I was asking her for different levels of work, but we never discussed her fee reflecting that. When we spoke, I proposed one fee for one kid, a higher fee for both, and yet another fee for when I needed housework and cooking. It was a bit complicated, but she shared how much more just this felt to her. In all her other jobs she got one fee and her employer would pile on extra work without paying her for it, and she felt resentful. She never felt comfortable saying anything about it, though. One of her employers was a friend of mine, so I asked her about this.

Her response was that since the babysitter didn't ask, it wasn't her responsibility to bring it up. I disagreed. There's a long history of domestic workers and other low-wage workers being disempowered and taken advantage of in our culture, so it makes sense that they don't feel able to advocate for themselves. That doesn't excuse those of us with the power from our responsibility.

REFLECTION

Are there areas in your life where you don't feel empowered to ask for what you need because of power dynamics? How might this contribute to your level of stress?

Are there areas of your life where others might feel that they cannot ask you for what they need because of power dynamics? What can you do to open up lines of communication with them?

Community Connections

I'm defining *community connections* here as people in our day-to-day lives who are not our family, colleagues, or chosen friends. This could be the person serving you at a restaurant or who you are serving, someone sitting in a waiting room with you, or someone working at a place you frequent. It can also include people in your neighborhood or in your workplace. Essentially, these are people who we don't have a deep relationship with and who we don't need to have much sustained interaction with on a regular basis. Yet these encounters can remind us of our shared humanity, even if it's just a quick glance or a smile at someone in line at the grocery store. We can feel connected without knowing someone very well. These types of connections can be simply based on a brief exchange or a mutual interest.

This is something I've had to learn to appreciate. I was never that person who chatted with my neighbors if I didn't feel I had anything in common with them. I never made small talk with the tellers at the bank or the person in front of me in line at the coffee shop. This is partly because as a young woman living in New York City, I got harassed a lot on the street. Being open to the people around me often resulted in getting catcalls and even being followed. I learned to shut down, put a scowl on my face, and walk around in the world defending against any unwanted attention. I was protecting myself. Also, growing up as an immigrant, I never saw my parents engaging in a meaningful way with people outside of our Lebanese friends. We stuck close to people who were like us because we didn't feel we had much in common with everyone else. Finally, as a very type A person, I also felt I never had time for these interactions; I've rushed through much of my life trying to meet my goals. One day, I heard someone ask, "What are you running toward so fast? Death?" I realized that my endless pursuit of efficiency was making me miss being in the moment. I was missing my life!

In the past few years I've been working on changing this and untangling myself from the various reasons I've disconnected from people in my outer circle. As I've aged, I'm no longer the object of unwanted stares and catcalls, so I feel safer being open to those around me I may not know well. Now I try and notice the people around me. I don't just stare at my phone when I'm in line at the coffee shop; I make myself put it away. I try and stand tall and smile at people. I'm not great at starting conversations with strangers, but I try to make it look like I'm available to have one if someone wanted to. Once in a while I push myself to make small talk. I'll compliment a cashier on her shirt or strike up a conversation at my kids' school with a parent I don't know well. I use my tools of grounding and breathing when I notice I'm anxious and want to find a way out of the conversation because I'm not sure what to say next. Much of my practice is about being okay with things feeling awkward, even if my heart is racing!

As I've worked on valuing interactions with the people I only meet in passing, I've noticed that those connections—with neighbors, cashiers, or my mail person—can be really sweet. Those interactions make the world feel kinder and warmer. More often than not, when I reach out to connect, the other person reciprocates. I try to not run through my day focused on my to-do list; I try to slow down and take in all the awesome people around me. I've taken such joy lately in bantering with my barista or remembering the UPS guy's name and that he loves dogs. The world feels smaller and more personal as a result. It's a nice antidote to the daily news, which mostly reports the ways we separate, divide, and hurt each other. You might find that, if you look for it, there are a lot of nice people out there ready to share a smile and some care.

Feeling connected to people we don't know well can be challenging, especially with people who are different from us. We may not feel we have the ability to have that warmth easily because we are unfamiliar with each other or, worse, we feel unsafe. Some of us are not able to assume that our efforts to reach out will be met with warmth and, of course, I'm not suggesting you should put yourself in harm's way. Yet, some of the kindest and most open people I know are people who have been targets of hate and bias for much of their life. They have let their hearts break open and are able to see the humanity in most people in a way that feels like a superhero power because they know how it feels to not be on the receiving end of warmth. They are still careful, of course, but often they are able to be disarming with their kindness and generosity. This can light up other peoples' desire for connection even if they have been masking it.

We all have different opportunities to extend our care outside of our immediate circle of core relationships. Care can look many ways. If you are someone who has the means, you may have people such as housekeepers and gardeners who work in your home. You likely have working-class people in your workplace, such as janitors and tradespeople. Very often those from higher socioeconomic backgrounds can forget about all the workers that make their lives comfortable. If this is you, reflect on some of these questions: Do you know how much the janitor gets paid? Do you know their name and if they have children? Do they get paid sick leave or have insurance? Are you thoughtful about how much you pay workers in your home? Do you pay them even when you travel and don't need their services? Do you know them personally? If you have children, are you raising them to have just as much respect for the workers in your life as they do for other adults? Care can look like paying someone an equitable wage and having concern and respect for them as a person. It doesn't mean you need to befriend all the workers in your life—they may not be interested in that—but notice if you don't give them the same regard as people you feel like you have more in common with.

People of all socioeconomic backgrounds can be thoughtful about those who help support us and make our lives more efficient and comfortable—everyone from bus and taxi drivers to grocery store and bank clerks to the folks who pick up our garbage. For many people it's easy to not see those who are in these roles, or to take them for granted. For others, it's impossible not to, because when you yourself work in the trades, service work, or the gig economy, you're more likely to have to rely on one another for resources and support.

Barriers to Connection

Many years ago, I volunteered to teach yoga in a program that helped people coming out of incarceration transition into the workforce. A group of young men were required to take my yoga class as part of this program. They weren't very happy about this. This particular group was impatient, uninterested, and sometimes flat-out rude. When I walked into class, there was usually one or two guys sitting on their mats smoking cigarettes; others were asleep or looking at their phones. During class, they barely did anything I suggested even though we talked about how stressful their lives were and how yoga could help with that. I was confused because, on one hand, they shared that they needed tools to deal with the anxiety of wanting to get their lives back on track, and on the other, they seemed annoyed at having to do the practice. I knew that all I could do was be kind and compassionate even though part of me felt impatient and irritable toward them. I had to remind myself that many of these young men had a history of adults in their life letting them down and even harming them. It made sense that they may not trust me yet. Many had spent their childhood in and out of incarceration and without adequate support and often getting messages that they were bad. I didn't want to replicate what they were used to—an authority figure getting mad at them and shaming them for their behavior. I always try to remember the idea that "the people who need love the most will ask for it in the most unloving ways." I held good boundaries, but I didn't shame them. I tried to remain warm and kind despite their lack of enthusiasm. I tried to remember that behind their defenses they probably wanted connection.

After a few weeks of showing up every Monday, I decided I needed to skip a week. I just wasn't feeling like I was having any impact, I was feeling defeated and needed a break. When I came back the following week, the students had made me cards. The cards featured pictures of us all doing yoga, and messages saying that they missed my good energy and were grateful for the class.

I remember thinking, "Who wrote these cards?" I could barely fathom that this uninterested group even noticed that I was gone. But they did. I realized that I *was* beginning to have an impact, but they simply weren't ready to show me yet. They weren't ready to let their guard down. How often had these young men let their guard down and gotten hurt? For them, it may have been unsafe to connect. They were going to reject me before I had the chance to reject them. Had I not realized this, I might have quit teaching them, and confirmed their belief that they can't get support, or that they will be let down and rejected.

There are many reasons we build barriers to connection. Usually it's fear of being rejected or hurt. Connection looks different for all of us—we all have different barriers to feeling safe with other people and different circumstances that we're dealing with. How others treat you is not always in your control, and some of us are swimming in more complicated or unsafe waters than others. Yet we all have, in our own way, the opportunity to practice building bridges to each other. If we don't, isolation becomes our prison, and fear the gatekeeper.

If I could speak to my younger self, I would tell her to see beyond people's veneer. To touch into her own vulnerability as a way to see others' vulnerability. I would tell her to prioritize kindness over being right, and to not use the excuse of being too busy to not be present with others. What would you tell your younger self?

REFLECTION

What are your barriers to connection to community? What small things can you do to shift this and open up?

Widening Your Circle of Compassion

Widening our circle of compassion also means considering the existence and well-being of people we don't know and may never know. These people and communities might be just a few blocks away or on the other side of the planet. Our lives are interconnected, which means that everything from the land we inhabit to the air we breathe, from the food we eat to the goods we produce or consume, connects us to other people and communities that are not visible to us. Similarly, their lives impact ours in ways we aren't aware of. When we make these invisible connections more visible, it can contribute to having peace from the part of our anxiety that is rooted in feeling isolated and disconnected. It can also help us make choices that tend to these connections in a conscious way.

As discussed previously, the myth of "rugged individualism" that is so valued in Western cultures encourages us to be out of relationship, and this actually can fuel our anxiety, because the truth is we exist within a web of rich relationships with other people, animals, and the land. To get curious about these invisible connections you might ask yourself about the history of the land you live on. What is your neighborhood like? Is it a gentrified or gentrifying area? Where does your electricity come from? How about your food? Are there farms in your area? Who has access to fresh food where you live, and who doesn't? Where are the major highways and factories in your area, and what is the history of how they were sited there? What are some of the communities surrounding you that you may not be aware of? What is their history and culture? What plants are native to your area? Can you find any in your neighborhood? (Hint: some may be growing out of the cracks in your sidewalk.) Are there community spaces near you? If you don't frequent them, find out who they serve and what their mission is.

As we tap into this less visible part of our connection ecosystem, we can start to feel like we're part of something bigger. We can also start to become aware of the ways that our actions—or inactions—can impact these other individuals and communities. It is important that we trace the impact of these choices and then act from a place of awareness. This allows us to shift out of dissociation and disconnection (which can be stressful) into active participation in a positive way. This can enrich our experience of connection and make our lives feel more meaningful and connected.

In my neighborhood in Venice Beach, California, there are lots of people without housing. Recently, a large encampment popped up a few blocks away from my house on a major road. Since a major cause of homelessness is a lack of affordable housing, I've done my best to get informed on the issue as it relates to the people in my community. This gives me the information I need so I can vote and support organizations that are addressing the root causes of the issue effectively. I also make it a point to walk over and bring food and supplies to the folks in the tents at least once a month. I use the opportunity to speak with them about their concerns and experience so I can learn from their perspective. When I shared this with my neighbor, she was shocked and afraid for me. She was all on board with donating and voting, but she admitted that when she goes by the tents she rolls up her windows and looks the other way.

I understand my neighbor's fear but, in my experience, most of the people I've approached have a lot to share and are glad to have someone who is listening. I will admit that for a while it was also my inclination to turn away when I passed the tents. I was afraid of what I might see if I looked, and I had no idea what I would say or do if someone tried to engage with me. When I began to think of these folks as people in my community, I started to approach them differently. I saw that many of these people were watching out for each other; they have built their own ecosystem of support that includes making sure everyone has food and blankets, watching each other's stuff so nothing gets stolen, and simply hanging out and being friends. Even though seeing people struggling with houselessness breaks my heart, knowing that Francine, who lives in her car with her dog, likes to feed him cat food, or that Jackson is out painting landscapes on scraps of wood because it settles his anxiety, humanizes the whole experience for me. I can hold both how traumatic it can be to be homeless with the resilience and perseverance that some of the folks I've met have. I used to think that looking away was a way to manage my anxiety, but the truth was quite the opposite. This is the tend-and-befriend response in action!

Where we put our money also impacts others. If you are in a position to change where you spend your money, you might think about purchasing products and food that are locally sourced and cultivated or made sustainably with ethical work practices and fair wages. You might also think about the social and ethical policies of where you bank or invest your money. What is your money being used for? Look for sustainable and ethical investment opportunities, find a socially responsible bank or ethical lender, invest in local business and businesses owned by people who have been historically marginalized. If changing how you spend your money isn't connected to relationship building, it may reduce your guilt, but it probably won't increase your feeling of connection and decrease your anxiety. So absolutely make different financial choices if you can, but don't think this is a replacement for building relationships. Do both!

As our world gets more and more globalized, we have invisible ties to people way beyond our local community. Part of our anxiety may be linked with this globalized nature of our existence and the ways that other people may be suffering as a result of our comfort.

I feel this every time I buy something that I suspect was made in a sweatshop abroad or when I fill my garbage bins to the brim. Knowing that we're complicit in supporting corporations and systems that don't treat their workers well or who are destroying the environment can exacerbate our anxiety and overwhelm. We can feel trapped because we know there's no way our individual choices alone will be enough to change this, since the problem is in the larger structures that we're a part of.

When we remember that connection is the key, we don't have to get overwhelmed with all that we can't control. As we become more aware of our interconnectedness, and as we actively engage in strengthening this web, we participate in healing ourselves and the wider communities of which we are a part. It's not about what brand of dish soap you buy or who makes your T-shirts, it's about understanding ourselves as part of a larger tapestry of life, and nurturing the strands of that web. As we widen our circle of compassion our hearts grow, and our capacity to love and live fully grows as well.

REFLECTION

What are one or two easy things you can do to widen your circle of compassion right away? What are one or two more challenging things you can work toward doing eventually? Set realistic goals for yourself and revisit this reflection periodically.

REFLECTION

Reflect on your connection ecosystem again. Consider going back to your original reflection and adding in potential new places to build and nurture connection that you may not have thought of before.

Connection to Self

Just like we cannot be whole without our connection to others intact, we cannot foster truly healthy relationships if we're not attending to our connection with ourselves. Being connected to ourselves requires us to be aware of ourselves—our soma (body), psyche (mind), and social location (the privileges and disadvantages we and our ancestors experienced). The first part of this book explored this. Understanding what we are bringing to an interaction can help us show up more authentically and truthfully. The famous psychiatrist Carl Jung said, "Until you make the unconscious conscious, it will direct your life and you will call it fate." Although not everything is simply a product of our unconscious thoughts and behaviors, it is important (and empowering) to know how our internal experiences impact our external world.

When it comes to your connection ecosystem, creating balance between your relationship with yourself and your relationship with others is essential. If you put most of your energy into yourself and skimp on your relationships with others, your ecosystem will suffer. However, if you put most of your energy into your relationships with others and skimp on attending to yourself, I suggest you get curious about that. Are you prioritizing your relationship with others to your own detriment? If so, you may want to ask yourself: what do relationships mean to you and what are your beliefs are about getting and maintaining connection in them? If you feel that you are somehow sacrificing yourself in order to get connection, your work might need to be about finding your own center and untangling yourself from unhealthy dynamics. Our need to feel connected and bonded to other people can be so strong that we will do whatever it takes to get it, especially if we have developmental trauma and didn't get the mirroring we needed as children from our caretakers. When we are not centered in a solid sense of self and self-worth, it can be hard to be in mutual relationships because we center our worth and sense of self in others. It's great to be generous and care for others, but it's just as important that we allow ourselves to receive the same care that we are so quick to give.

My friend Layla is a giver. Her day job is as a social worker working in child protective services. She is a single mom of two and a therapeutic foster parent, which means that she takes in children with trauma and mental health conditions until they are placed in a permanent home. Oh—and she has four dogs, three cats, and an iguana (all rescues). She is the kind of person who puts everyone first; she's there for every crisis or celebration. She'll drop everything to help a friend or even a stranger. Her relationships are the most important thing to her. The other day I saw Layla after a very intense day at work where she had to remove two small kids from a very violent household, and the father threatened her, so she had to call the police. She was late to meet me because she stopped by the animal shelter on her way home to see if there were any new animals that were scheduled to be euthanized. When I saw her, she was visibly shaking, but that didn't stop her from wanting to make us dinner. When I told her she should sit and I could do the cooking, she refused. She insisted that she was very particular about her kitchen and no one was allowed to cook or even clean except her.

Layla is stubborn and strong-willed. It's really hard to find ways to support her that she will accept. I know her history and that she had to take care of her siblings growing up because her mother had an untreated mental health condition. Layla protected her younger siblings from her mom's attacks, and one day she fell asleep in the afternoon out of sheer exhaustion. While she was asleep, her mom beat her little brother so badly he got a black eye. Layla never forgave herself for not being there to protect him. For her, rest was associated with other people getting hurt. As you can see, she recreated a life where there is little room for rest and she spends most of her energy protecting vulnerable children and animals. She worked herself to the bone and it's no surprise that at forty-two she was diagnosed with chronic fatigue syndrome. Her body shut down on her and forced her to slow down. She had to make some drastic changes in her life. She had to ask for help because she literally couldn't do everything on her own alone anymore.

For some of us, letting our guard down and receiving support from others may be associated with unsafe situations where we were hurt or abused. We may be unconsciously defending against those feelings by doing things for others. The doing can be an attempt to feel in control and manage our anxiety, but, as you can see with Layla, if we don't acknowledge what is truly going on, we can literally make ourselves sick. Some of us are not as extreme as Layla, but, in our own way, we use prioritizing others as a defense. If you feel you have a lot of people around you but you feel anxious or alone, you might ask yourself this question: what is scary about letting go and receiving from others?

REFLECTION

Are you a giver in relationships? If so, how does it feel for you when you receive? What emotions or impulses come up for you? Is there anything scary about receiving in your relationships?

Solitude

Cultivating a strong relationship with yourself and your interior world is a cornerstone of relating to others in a healthy way.

When relationships are an escape from the self, they can never be satisfying. Solitude—spending time alone intentionally—can be one way to build your relationship with yourself. This can look like a quiet walk in nature, meditation, journaling, or even making art. This is not about doing things like cleaning your house, watching Netflix, or working on your taxes. When we can't stand to be alone, we can sometimes use things like substances, tasks, or people to distract us from ourselves.

Our ability to be alone with our thoughts with curiosity and compassion is one aspect of solitude. So is our capacity to not be distracted—to simply be in the moment. Admittedly, this is getting harder and harder as most of us have in the palm of our hand access to infinite entertainment and stimulation. In the book *Digital Minimalism*, Cal Newport defines solitude as "a subjective state in which your mind is free from input from other minds."[4] He says that with the advent of the iPod and then the quick rollout of the smartphone and all its apps, many people had the option to be continually distracted from their own minds.

It can be hard to practice solitude when we are so used to continual stimulation and distraction. If you want to build this muscle, start small: designate three to five minutes at some point every day to simply sit, or walk, without your phone or any stimulation. Gradually increase the time. You can even do it while you're in a waiting room or a cab—simply turn off your phone, put down a book or magazine, and just be. Then try to look for other opportunities during your day that you might normally fill with stimulation out of habit, and practice solitude instead. As you get comfortable with this, you can expand your time—maybe have a meal alone in a quiet place or spend longer amounts of time in nature or in meditation.

MEDITATION PRACTICE: BEING A FRIEND TO YOURSELF

Find a place to sit comfortably. You can practice grounding or breathing or even do a few stretches first. Once you feel settled, imagine sitting with yourself as you would sit with someone you care about deeply. Try to connect with a feeling of compassion and curious presence without an agenda. Try this for at least five minutes.

REFLECTION

Do you have solitude in your life? How does it look? What can you do to have more solitude?

UNPLUGGING FROM TECHNOLOGY PRACTICE

Plan to take some time away from your phone daily, or weekly. Consider taking a walk without it, eating a meal without it, or even taking a full- or half-day break from it.

Solitude, unlike loneliness, is when we choose to be alone. Solitude can give us the space to cultivate a positive relationship with ourselves. When we like ourselves, it's easier to believe that others can as well. As I said in the beginning of this chapter, this does not have to come first. Liking and loving ourselves can come through relationships and how we learn and grow in them. Regardless of the order, healthy relationships with others and with ourselves are both important to feeling connected.

8

Connecting with Something Bigger

Reclaiming Wonder

I'LL SAY IT again: connection is the key to releasing our anxiety and being well. Connection to ourselves, by understanding our own psyche and nervous system; connection to other people; and, finally, we need connection to something bigger than us. Some of us think of this as God, Allah, or Spirit. Some of us think of this as the Great Mystery, Nature, or Beloved Community. I sometimes think of this as a nervous system state. Ultimately this thing is ineffable—hard to describe with words. It can feel sacred, like it carries meaning beyond what we can rationally understand. I see it as a feeling that we are part of a larger order of things that has nothing to do with us and everything to do with us. It's a feeling of awe.

I believe that we can be grounded in reality and open to astonishment. Magic and pragmatism aren't mutually exclusive. This is where my path has taken me. But I wasn't always this way.

In my youth, up until my twenties, I did a lot of magical thinking. This is when we attribute a causal relationship between our thoughts and actions to external events. I always tried to see the upside of situations, and I believed that I "manifested" things that came into my life in order to learn important lessons.

I tended to interpret events in a metaphysical way, as if they transcended the laws of nature and were orchestrated by the universe to give me a specific experience that I needed to have. This was my attempt to manage my anxiety about all that was out of my control. I never had to feel worried about what might happen because I "knew" that whatever it was, there was reason and purpose to it.

One day I made a new friend, Julian Walker, whose perspective on life challenged many of my beliefs.[1] Julian was a yoga teacher interested in ecstatic dance, healing, and psychology like I was. We had a lot in common. He was a very passionate, soulful, and creative person, and I was surprised to learn that he identified as an atheist. In fact, he was very passionate about the idea that we can cultivate ecstatic states of being without attributing the experience to a higher power or spiritual belief system. Julian would often challenge my worldview and invite me to see things more practically than I tended to. For example, one day I shared with him that I had had a really special day. I described to him all the synchronicities of bumping into several people I knew in my neighborhood while taking a walk. One person happened to have a book I'd been wanting to read in his hands, and he gave it to me. The other person offered me a job teaching yoga at her studio. In my mind, things felt so positive and magical that I could only explain them by saying that there was some higher power orchestrating these events on my behalf. (I also had a similar habit of explaining bad stuff, like my dysplasia diagnosis.)

Julian gently reflected back to me that maybe this wasn't some magical series of events. Maybe I'm just a nice person who knows a lot of people in my neighborhood. Maybe I have enough good rapport with folks such that when I bump into them, they are going to have positive things to share with me. Oh—and that book I was hoping to get my hands on was a current best seller, so the chances that someone I knew had it were high. Maybe this wasn't magic but the power of my strong relationships and yoga-teaching skills. I began to see that he might be right—that there were very plausible psychological and practical explanations for my experiences. Just because they felt magical to me didn't mean that they literally were. And I didn't need a metaphysical explanation to tap into the feeling of wonder inspired by a day that felt so fortuitous.

I began to see the limitations of my overly optimistic viewpoint. The problem was that I had to do a lot of mental gymnastics to maintain this perspective in certain situations, like when I had an unexpected miscarriage or when I heard about the violence and oppression others have to endure. These things didn't have an obvious upside, and to think that other people "manifested" their dire circumstances just wasn't fair. My belief system didn't have room for random, bad events to occur, and it certainly didn't have room for including the inequality and oppression many groups of people face. As someone with access to resources—I lived in a clean, safe place, had enough money to cover my basic needs, and chose a career that I had training and opportunity in—I didn't have to confront too many things in my daily life that challenged my rosy views. I also kept my life small: I mostly interacted with people like me, and I avoided getting involved in politics or reading the news ("such negative energy"). I created a reality that didn't test me too much; I lived in an echo chamber of like-minded people with similar lifestyles and values.

I realized that if I wanted to be whole, I had to expand my awareness and cultivate a worldview that included things like random bad things happening, political violence, discrimination, and oppression. I had to let go of the idea that we create our reality, and everything is a product of our own beliefs and thoughts. I had to let go of magical thinking. I had to find a way to embrace *all* of life more honestly and fully—the beautiful parts and the difficult parts that I can't make sense of.

For many people, believing in a higher power has nothing to do with magical thinking—such beliefs often support resilience in the face of difficulty, rather than bypass. But for me, magical thinking was tied to my desire to bypass difficulty, and it was important for me to detox from this tendency. As I did with many things that I became interested in, I embraced this idea full force: I started reading the news and learning more about what was happening in the world outside of my comfortable bubble. I pooh-poohed any positive thinking as naive and superficial. I stopped attending group gatherings that involved music and ritual because many of the people there held beliefs I was no longer cool with. I went to the opposite extreme and became a poster child for skepticism and pragmatism. At first this was a good move. It forced me to confront the emotions I had denied by throwing fairy dust on them. It broke my habit of bypassing difficult feelings to get to the lesson or happy ending. It also made me confront parts of myself that I pretended didn't exist (like my angry side and my judgmental side). But after several years of skeptical atheism, I started to feel anxious—really anxious. Part of my anxiety was tied to this new way of thinking. Since I no longer believed that everything had a larger meaning or purpose anymore, everything felt random. I became preoccupied with fear and worry about the future. I didn't trust that there was some greater flow or meaning to life. Things felt fragile and haphazard, like something terrible could happen any moment. My old beliefs had buffered me from this vulnerability, and now I was overwhelmed by it. Everything felt out of control and I had no idea how to manage it. I was also having to confront and work through this feeling of vulnerability that I had defended against all of my life. I had to feel my fear full force in order for it to not overcome me. It sucked.

In order to deal with my anxiety, I had to allow myself to reconnect to aspects of my old belief system in a healthier way. I missed the part of me that could find greater meaning in suffering and challenge. This helped me face difficulty with greater confidence and resolve. I missed the inspiration and guidance I could get from tarot cards and my dreams. I missed my altar, my special crystal and objects that anchored particular memories and feelings. I really missed the group gatherings of music and ritual that had been a big part of my life before. My commitment to acknowledging my vulnerability and humanity did help me become more integrated and realistic, but it left something lacking. Life felt like a meal that was underseasoned. I wanted that flavor back, and I had to figure out how to do it without returning to old habits that were more about avoidance and denial than about recognizing the interconnectedness of life and the beauty and solace we can find in that. When I'd let go of magical thinking, I'd inadvertently let go of all the other ways I could access a feeling of meaning and wonder. I had to reclaim this if I was going to feel whole and good again.

As I opened up to a more grounded attitude, I was able to participate in group rituals and understand that being in community while dancing, singing, or even meditating can create a feeling of magic and unexplainable beauty and meaning. The thing is, it *is* explainable. It's called *entrainment*—this is our tendency to sync up with each other through our breath and heart rate during group experiences like this. We enter a brain and body state of feeling connected, and it's powerful! Magical! Also, simply sitting and sharing in a group of trusted people in a ritual way is a potent experience that can shift our perspective and inspire healing. The emotional support and mirroring we get can help us access parts of ourselves that we can't alone or in a one-on-one interaction. Before I met my husband, I participated in a ritual circle with two close friends. I brought a candle and some sage and we meditated together for a bit. Then I shared with them that I was ready for partnership and open to meeting the right man. I spoke about what I wanted and what kind of a person I hoped to be with. They were very supportive and told me that I deserved to find a loving partner and that they were rooting for me.

Two weeks later I met Paul! Was it magic? It certainly felt like it. But the more likely explanation is that because I was conscious that I wanted a partner, I was open when a friend said she had someone she wanted to set me up with. When I met Paul, instead of acting aloof and disinterested, as I normally might have, I was warm and kind. This is probably why he asked me out. I should also mention that I did this ritual with my friends after lots of therapy, self-reflection, and awareness of why I wanted to be in relationship. I did years of work to feel ready to be open to a healthy relationship. Having my friends witness and hold my desire felt sacred. It gave me that extra bit of confidence and support to open up to what I wanted and to take action when the opportunity arose.

For me, reclaiming wonder is about staying grounded in reality while still feeling connected to something ineffable and unexplainable. "Wonder" is defined by the *Oxford English Dictionary* as "a feeling of surprise mingled with admiration, caused by something beautiful, unexpected, unfamiliar or inexplicable." This is about opening ourselves up to an experience of something we cannot explain that makes things meaningful and allows us to feel connected to all of life. This "thing" may be neurotransmitters in our brain getting stimulated, the Collective Unconscious, Love, Nature, Spirit, the Universe, God, or something else. The important thing isn't what we name it, it's the fact that we need this connection to something bigger in order to feel held and supported. Reclaiming wonder can be the key to accessing this. This can be done in many ways; this chapter ends with a list of ideas and ways to tap into this state.

Connection to Something Bigger

Finding healthy and grounded ways to connect to the mystery of life can help us cope with our anxiety and stress, and it can help us find meaning, joy, and delight. It's important to be grounded in reality and deal with our shit, but this doesn't mean we give up experiences that touch the fantastical, nonrational parts of ourselves. I like the metaphor of the tree here: if a tree is to get closer to the light (the sun), it has to dig its roots deep into the dirt. We too need to dig into our dirt and darkness to access our light. There's nutrition in that dirt; when we avoid it, we can't flourish. We don't tell a tree that it's impractical or unrealistic because it's reaching for the sky—its reaching is a sign of health. As humans, we can let our work of acknowledging our own darkness fuel our openness to the beauty and splendor of life.

Andy Fisher, author of *Radical Ecopsychology*, talks about our need to be connected to nature because it provides us with a larger context to hold our suffering. He says that "to stay above the healing threshold we need a context for containing our pain that is larger or stronger than the pain itself."[2] When we don't feel connected to something bigger than our pain, our pain overcomes us and we focus more on strategies to avoid pain rather than embracing life to its fullest.

There are lots of ways to experience this connection with something bigger than ourselves. You might already have beliefs and rituals that help you do this, you might be questioning your current beliefs, or you might not have any rituals or beliefs that feel meaningful. I encourage you to give some of the suggestions below a try even if you already have some practices in place. See which ones resonate for you. One thing is for sure: this is not an intellectual endeavor; it's experiential. It's not something we can just think about or study. A point of view that goes beyond what we can rationally wrap our minds around can offer perspective and clarity. I think that the most settling and reassuring feeling state we can cultivate is that of knowing we're not separate from anything, that we are held in this larger web of life. So, whatever we call it, *it* is this thing that reminds us of our true nature—which is that we are deeply and intrinsically connected. This thing allows us to see each other as part of a larger whole. Everyone equally valuable and lovable.

To explore this idea in a different way, take a moment to contemplate its opposite. Think of a moment when you felt particularly terrible—anxious, depressed, lonely, or apathetic. I bet that in that moment you felt supremely alone, unsupported, or disconnected. I bet in that moment you felt separate and like life had no meaning. If separation is the disease, connection is the cure. Finding ways to connect to something bigger serves to remind us that we are part of something and that we are not alone. It can help us make sense of our suffering as well. It's easy to let our life be a series of tasks and responsibilities where we are rushing from one thing to the next. When we take time to pause and feel into the ineffable, it can give us perspective and a sense of meaning, even awe.

REFLECTION

Do you have a relationship to something bigger than you? How do you access wonder? If you don't, how might you cultivate this connection? Write or draw your answer.

Religion is an obvious way that some people connect and make meaning beyond what we can prove. Religious rituals and communities can be a tremendous source of support for people during difficult times as well as during celebratory times. Religion—both the institutions and the beliefs—can also perpetuate denial. Some religious beliefs can be a bypass that explain away or keep you from confronting your real fears and pain, like my magical thinking was earlier in life. I had a friend who was a devout Catholic. When she got diagnosed with stage 4 breast cancer that had spread to her lungs, she held on tightly to the notion that God wouldn't let anything bad happen to her. She prayed and prayed for healing and refused to acknowledge that she might die. When it became clear that there was no cure and she only had a few weeks to live, she was angry at God. She felt betrayed, and she died kicking and screaming, refusing to accept her fate. It was a painful experience for all who knew her to see our friend not just facing death but feeling abandoned by a God she had trusted her whole life. Many Catholics have room in their beliefs for facing the tragedies of life, but this friend of mine did not. I've seen people transformed by the dying process (their own and others'). Their healing did not come in the form of a cure, but in facing death as a meaningful process in and of itself. They didn't have to believe in an afterlife to have a sacred experience of dying. If our beliefs can't help us be with suffering in a meaningful way, they are not that useful when push comes to shove.

The Web of Life

Wonder can touch us into knowing that we're a part of the web of life in a way that is beyond the intellect. It's a feeling that we are all connected in a meaningful and vital way. This is particularly hard these days—our modern lives insulate us from the direct experience of many of the things that sustain us and are a natural part of life. Our ancestors grew their own food, hunted the animals they ate, made their clothes, and knew all the people in their tribe. They witnessed birth, death, and illness firsthand. Just two generations ago, most people lived in towns or neighborhoods where they knew many of the inhabitants. They shopped at their local butcher or produce store, where they knew the owners and maybe even the farmers. Most of us today have no idea where our food comes from. Our meat comes neatly plastic-wrapped and covered in fake images of happy animals on a family farm. Many of our fruits and vegetables are grown far away from where we live and are shipped to us by workers who don't get a fair wage. We may not know the history of the land we live on or have any relationships with our neighbors. We may not have a direct experience of the seasons—we can eat most foods year-round and many of us live in temperature-controlled spaces with artificial lights, protected from the weather.

Many of us are also insulated from direct experiences of birth and death—two things that are mostly relegated to hospitals and specialists. In the United States we put many elderly people in nursing homes, our babies and children are not typically allowed in adult spaces, and neurodivergent people and people with disabilities and mental health conditions are segregated from "normal" society. Our lives are so sanitized, organized, and "civilized" that anything that disrupts this illusion of order becomes marginalized. Our obsession with convenience has some side effects that are not so good for the soul.

Western culture, for all its amazing advancements in science, philosophy, and technology, has not historically had the foresight to know when to curb its obsession with efficiency, progress, and growth. We think we can control nature, and our environmental crisis is a symptom of this lack of reverence and respect for the entire ecosystem that humans are only one part of. Our culture's insatiable appetite for fossil fuels is gutting the Earth and causing changes in climate that may cause the end of the human species. The illusion that we are separate from the Earth is suicide. Not only is it dangerous on a practical, physical level, it is killing our souls by separating us from the very thing that sustains us and holds us.

Apathy and Overwhelm

I invite you to pause and notice what you feel when you read the previous paragraph about the human impact on the environment. Do you want to defend? Do you feel totally defeated? Are you inspired? When faced with the massiveness of all of the challenges in the world, many of us might want to throw in the towel and give up hope and become apathetic. Or we might minimize the gravity of the situation. We might decide to just focus on our individual needs. Maybe we extend our care out to our family and friends; the rest is just too much. The problem is, when we throw in the towel, we disconnect from that larger-than-us thing—nature, God, whatever your name for it is.

Some people and communities don't have the luxury to be in denial because they bear the brunt of the negative side effects of environmental unsustainability. Poor communities (typically made up of people of color) are where the most polluting factories and highways are located. The water, air, and soil are toxic, and the rates of cancer, cardiovascular disease, and premature death are higher in these communities than in affluent ones. For people in economic survival mode who are directly impacted by a system that values profit over environmental sustainability, addressing this is a matter of life or death. In this case, a connection to something bigger can also be a vital source of support and hope. I know many activists who come from communities directly impacted by systems of greed and oppression who are fueled by their commitment to a bigger vision of collective healing and justice. They are deeply connected to a sense of spirituality and wonder that allows them to access a feeling of optimism even in a world of pain and suffering.

The question is not whether or not you can live a perfect life dedicated to environmental sustainability and justice for all. The question is, are you willing to risk hope? Even if you won't see any results in your lifetime, can you live a life that can contribute to setting the conditions right for future generations? When we live our life connected to the sacred in some way, we broaden our awareness, live beyond the immediate moment, and let go of our individual, narcissistic need for gratification. When we live a life embedded in the sacred, it can make us happier. It can allow life to feel more meaningful and expansive. Even if trying to live sustainably or spending time in prayer or in nature doesn't make a huge impact on the outside world, it can make an impact on your inside world. I believe that if we all lived in a way where we did our best to leave a world to the next generation that is more equitable and just, everyone would benefit.

Connecting with Nature

Ecopsychology studies the relationship between humans and the natural world. It suggests that much of our anxiety and pain is rooted in our disconnection from nature. One author, Chellis Glendinning, an ecopsychologist and trauma therapist, says that our disconnection from the natural world is the equivalent of a child being taken away from its mother—it's traumatic to all of us to not feel held by the natural rhythms of life. We may not be conscious of it, for many of us never knew this connection, but it causes us disruption and dysregulation nonetheless.

Spending time in nature can be a powerful way to not just regulate our nervous system but also experience our interconnection to something bigger than us (which also regulates our nervous system!). I've always wanted to be more of a nature person—someone who goes camping or can sit in the woods for hours marveling in awe at the trees. I want to be someone who consistently has dirt under their nails from being in the garden. The truth is, I can't keep a houseplant alive. I love to hike, but usually, if I'm honest, I do it because the exercise feels good. I like camping, but I'm kind of scared of bugs and wild animals. Yet, even with my limitations, I have had profound moments in nature. One of these moments was in college. This stands out because back then, I didn't meditate or do yoga, and I didn't have a grasp of myself like I do now. My mind was like a crowded bus station filled with people scurrying about bumping into each other trying to get nowhere. It was overwhelming in there, and I didn't have the tools yet to deal with it. But when I was forced to be still, and I was in a quiet setting, I was able to tap into a serenity that I didn't have words for.

One spring, a group of us went out to Long Island, where one of my friend's parents had a house, for the weekend. Aside from a drunken game of truth or dare (which I only recall parts of) I distinctly remember an experience I had sitting by a tree on the first day. I arrived early at the house, and I had no choice but to sit down in his beautiful garden and wait for him to arrive. Back then I couldn't distract myself with a smartphone. It was just me, my thoughts, and the trees. I was forced into stillness. In that stillness something happened that I couldn't describe. At first, my mind got amped up with anxiety. Without any distraction, the chatter was louder than usual. I regretted not bringing a book or some homework to catch up on. Time was going by so slowly. When would my friend arrive?! Then I lay down and began watching some ants climbing up the tree trunk. The texture of the trunk was so interesting, and I started to contemplate the smallness of humanity crawling on this big Earth like those ants. Then I noticed the way the leaves shimmered in the sunlight and, when the wind came, they all shimmied in unison.

I became awestruck. I'm not sure why. It was more of a feeling than a thought. A feeling of being connected to that tree and its dancing leaves. A feeling of how small my worries were when embedded in the larger ecosystem of the natural world. A connection to a larger logic and rhythm that had nothing to do with me as an individual but had a wisdom of its own. I remember dropping into a quality of presence that was new. Some might say I was present to the divine, others might say my nervous system became more regulated and my brain produced neurochemicals that made me feel good. Whatever you call it, the feeling is one that is somewhat magical. I was tapping into an energy and rhythm larger than me. I felt held; I felt safe.

We Need to Disconnect to Connect

These days, if I'm not careful, I won't have any moments like the one I just described. I don't ever have to sit still and just stare at the world unless I choose to. This is because I have in the palm of my hand a smartphone that gives me around-the-clock access to distraction. This is true for many of us. If you want to live life connected to the larger mystery of life, you must spend time disconnected from the Internet and too much stimulation. Too much stimulation desensitizes us from noticing the subtle things that can touch us into wonder. I remember hearing a comedian describe a scene by a river with his teenage son. The boy is glued to his phone scrolling through videos when the father spots a bear catching a salmon in his mouth. He yells to the boy to look, and the boy glances up from the phone, sees the bear, shrugs, and goes back to browsing. When we get used to getting entertained by memes and sound bites, we lose the ability to tolerate slower forms of stimulation and to appreciate simple things.

If I'm really honest, I fight the urge to check my phone in moments of forced stillness, like in line at the store or even at a red light. I have to work hard to read entire books and long articles. I have to actively fight to be in control of what gets my attention; if I don't, my devices will monopolize it. Tristan Harris, a former Google engineer, has become a whistleblower on how technology is designed to get our attention and keep it. This is how the technology industry makes money. Technology is not neutral. It wants a monopoly on our attention. We may think we're in control, but for many of us—especially children exposed to digital media from a young age—our brains are being shaped by apps and functions designed to hook into our anxiety and keep us scrolling.

Recently, I discovered part of the science behind this. Texting, scrolling through social media, and playing video games can all be quick ways to get a dose of dopamine, which feels good—in the moment. Dopamine is known to cause *seeking* behaviors. It makes you curious about things and motivates you to look for more information or stimulation. (Sometimes we get stuck in a "dopamine loop" where we have a hard time stopping that seeking behavior. This happens when we can't stop scrolling through Facebook or checking our notifications.) Speaking to someone in person (or even on the phone), on the other hand, can produce oxytocin, which gives us a good feeling related to trust, bonding, and connection. It doesn't trigger more seeking of pleasure; rather, it gives us the feeling of actual pleasure. When we are able to experience a real sense of connection, it shifts our nervous system and brain into a state of equilibrium and ease rather than anxiety about getting our next hit of pleasure.

Rituals of Connection

Rituals of connection are things that we do with the explicit intention to tap into the experience of wonder and presence with something bigger than us. Regardless of the activity, having the intention to touch into the sacred is important. It can turn the most mundane activity into something special. For some of us, these rituals are common practice, such as religious services, creative activities like dance or music, or prayer and meditation. You might come from a culture rich in these rituals; if so, keep them up if they are meaningful for you.

If you don't have particularly poignant rituals that you practice, here are some ideas. Even if you do have practices of your own, try some of these to see if they might complement or add to your experience.

Nature
Being in Nature is one great way to remember that we are part of something bigger than ourselves. If you have a chance to get out on a hike or go to a beautiful location and just sit, that's great. You can also connect with nature in parks or even by paying new attention to the plants, clouds, or creatures around where you live. We can find nature almost everywhere—it's not just in protected landscapes, it's growing out of the cracks in the sidewalks and in houseplants. Make sure that you actually let yourself take in the environment. Consider leaving your phone behind, and if you're

walking, go slow. Set the intention to be present and take in your surroundings. Don't get too caught up in needing to have some mystical or magical experience; just practice being present. If this is a new practice, you might find that you have a low tolerance, and after fifteen or twenty minutes you might be ready to check emails on your phone or get back to civilization. If you make it a habit, your nervous system will start to recalibrate. You'll find that each time you can stay a bit longer and you won't crave your usual distractions as much.

I've gotten in the habit of sitting in my backyard watching bees. After a few minutes, I feel mesmerized by them, and amazed at how active yet peaceful they are. My family has also gotten into the habit of going on family picnics at the local park. You don't have to be at the Grand Canyon or Yosemite to connect to nature. In *To Be Healed by the Earth*, Warren Grossman suggests meditating while looking at a houseplant.[3] He reminds us that nature is everywhere, not just in pristine areas separated from everything else.

Movement

Walking, wheeling, scootering, or any kind of movement is a great way to get into a state of presence and connection. It's like a moving meditation of sorts. In the Buddhist tradition a walking meditation is done by walking very slowly and paying attention to the sensation of your feet contacting the ground. Many Indigenous traditions have walking rituals. It's been proven that walking is great for physical and mental health and that even ten minutes of walking or movement a day can have a significant impact on both.

Walking as a ritual of connection just requires you to do a few things: reject distractions like cell phones, don't be in a hurry to get anywhere, and ideally be in a pleasant setting. Remember, it's the intention that matters. Although not ideal, I bet you could do a walking meditation in a mall with the intention to connect to something bigger. Maybe you could gaze at all the people around you with deep love and reverence. If you go slow and move consciously, who says the mall can't be sacred? Nature is an obvious first choice for a walk like this. I like to walk around my neighborhood taking in the different plants in people's lawns. I make it a point to smile at the people I pass too. I leave my phone at home, or I listen to inspiring music and put my phone on "do not disturb." The hardest part for me is slowing down my pace, both physically and mentally.

Dancing

Dance is one of the most ancient forms of ritual. You don't have to be "good" at it. I'm not talking about dance as a performance but dance as an experience. This is not about learning choreography; it's about tapping into a rhythm in your body. If this is a new concept to you, put on a song with some rhythm, preferably some drums, and just find one movement and repeat it a bunch of times, then do another movement and repeat. You can do this whether you're able-bodied or you have limited mobility. Some of my friends in wheelchairs can get their groove on more passionately than my friends who are professional dancers.

Singing

My dear friend and colleague Suzanne Sterling is a powerful healer and singer whose work is helping people find their voice.[4] She says that she's never met a person who can't sing. We might not know how to use our instrument, but we can all sing, she often reassures us. She encourages people to take their singing out of their showers and cars and sing together. Rituals of collective singing are single-handedly some of the most powerful rituals

I've ever experienced. Try it. If you're mortified at the idea of singing or chanting in a group, use your somatic tools to keep you grounded so you can try it. Many of us were told not to sing or be loud at some point in our lives, which can make it even harder to freely make sound. Whenever Suzanne and I teach together, and I sing with the group, I will inevitably find myself in tears. Tears of joy, tears of grief, and tears that just feel like a release of something. Sometimes they feel like tears of remembering.

Circles of Connection

Being with friends is one thing, but if you sit in a circle and are deliberate about your time together, it can shift the experience and help you tap into something special. Circles of storytelling, ritual, and governance have been a part of many cultures worldwide for millennia. This may sound simple, but it can be quite profound. For example, a practice called council has its roots in many different Native American and First Nations peoples, and has been respectfully adapted for use in the fields of mediation, restorative justice, and others. In a council, people sit in a circle so they can connect in a ritualized way. The group passes around a talking piece such as a stone, stick, or any special object, and whoever has the piece can speak. Everyone else simply listens without commentary. In some circles, people use their time to check in and share how they are doing. Sometimes the group sets a particular theme and folks respond to a specific question or prompt.

I've done parenting circles with friends where we check in about our process as parents. After the initial go-around, the circle usually shifts into an organic conversation where there is more of a back-and-forth. This is very different than just having everyone come over to hang out without structure. Circles of connection are done with the explicit intention of fostering connections and hearing and seeing each other. They are not necessarily about solving a problem or giving advice; they are about listening and witnessing. Circles can also be done to address issues or conflict between people, but those usually require a skilled facilitator. Use circles with caution if there are contentious or unresolved dynamics between participants.

You might have access to circles held by other people where you live. I live in Los Angeles where there is an abundance of drum circles, goddess circles, healing circles, and so forth. Most of them are groups of sincere people who want to build community and connection, although it's important to be aware of the small percentage who are led by manipulative leaders who misuse their power. Look for people who simply want to bring people together and recognize that the magic is in our collective intention and connection to each other.

Spiritual Practice

Spiritual practices such as prayer, chanting, and going to church, temple, or mosque can all be rituals of connection. Whatever you choose, let it be meaningful to you. You may have access to practices that are part of traditions you did not grow up in, such as sweat lodges or medicine journeys. These can be transformative, but they also run the risk of being exploitative or appropriating. Before engaging in such rituals, I urge you to make sure the facilitators are sincere and come from the culture that the tradition is a part of.

You can create your own simple rituals like making a small altar space where you can place meaningful objects, light a candle, and use it as a space for meditation or reflection. Creating a sacred space in your home—a place meant to be intentional and meaningful—can be a powerful way to build ritual into your life. Spiritual practice doesn't have to be religious. My kids both have altars in their room. Their altars include objects that are meaningful to them—a rock from a river we visit often, pictures of friends, sports pins, and even pretty candy wrappers from the candy shop we go to when we visit their cousins. They don't sit and meditate in front of their altars (I wish they did), but it is a place that anchors meaningful things for them.

Making Art

For many of us, art is something to be observed or consumed, not made. If we're not "good" at it, we shy away from doing it. But making art, whether it's a painting, a sculpture, or music, can be a healing process regardless of the final product. Research has found that the simple act of coloring puts the brain in a similar state to meditation. I am not super crafty, but I know that each time I sit with my eight-year-old and build Legos or color, if I let myself get into it, I get transported. I'm not saying that Legos will connect you with the sacred (well, maybe I am), but it can change your state to one that is more present.

Another thing my friend Suzanne says is that "entertainment is killing us." She likes to remind us that we are all artists. It's our nature to create! Somehow in the last few generations making art has been relegated to people who identify as or train to be artists. The rest of us then sit back and watch. Many people before us (and today) danced, made music, and created together as part of their daily rituals—not because they were professionals entertaining others.

Traveling

Traveling to new places and cultures can be one way to break the monotony of everyday life and remember that we are connected to a much larger world. Travel isn't affordable for everyone, but if you can do it, get yourself out of your comfort zone once in a while and explore a different landscape or culture. Even making time to visit places in your town that you don't normally go or exploring somewhere just a few hours away can be inspiring.

Several times in my life I've purchased a plane ticket and a guidebook and embarked on an unplanned adventure. These experiences shaped me and my perspective of the world. I got to know new people and places that were so different from what I was used to at home. During my travels, I took local transportation whenever possible, stayed at hostels, and ate at local restaurants serving authentic cuisine from the area. When we are in a new place, we can see things through a new lens. We don't take our surroundings for granted, and there's a quality of presence we find ourselves in that differs from when we are in our familiar surroundings.

If you are someone who can afford travel where everything is planned out and you are perfectly comfortable, consider letting some of that go and engaging with your surroundings rather than just being a spectator. Get off the tour bus or leave the museum presentation and let yourself wander in awe of your surroundings and curious about the lived experience of the residents. Don't just be a spectator in this new place—participate. Leave room for magic. Let traveling disrupt what you know; let it open you up. You don't have to go anywhere exotic to have this experience.

PRACTICE: YOUR RITUALS OF CONNECTION

Create your rituals of connection: Pick one or two of the ideas above and try them in the next week or two. Reflect on the impact they had, and which ones can become more regular practices in your life.

Intention

Remember, your intention is key. Almost any activity can be connecting if you want it to be. We can experience the sacred in any moment. In fact, part of resacralizing our world is softening the boundary between the mundane aspects of life and the sacred and special parts. If we can only feel connected when conditions are perfectly set up for it, we'll rarely feel it. Chances to connect are everywhere; we just have to look for them.

I can't tell you which level of connection is the most important —with yourself, with others, or with something bigger. I just know it's hard to feel whole and happy without all of them. I have clients who have unmanageable PTSD and their internal GPS is so off that they can't take in the support that exists around them, and it's really hard to tap into the ineffable when alarm bells are constantly ringing in your body. I know people who have a serious commitment to self-care—good nutrition, yoga or meditation, and rest—but they still feel sad and alone. In fact, their loneliness can serve to increase their neuroticism and self-obsession. I also know people with very dedicated spiritual beliefs and practices who don't take care of themselves and are sick and burnt-out because they are caring for everyone else. In order to be whole, we need to examine and find health in all these aspects of ourselves.

9

The Global Heart

Redefining Self

THERE IS A collective anxiety that many people are experiencing these days. It's an anxiety about the state of the world—politics, the environment, lack of safety in public spaces, our relationship to people different from us. For some people, this is not new, and for others it is a disruption of a feeling of peace and stability that they've been accustomed to. So, whether you just got to the collective anxiety party or you and your community have been here for generations, it's undeniable that right now, at the time of the writing of this book, there is a sense of unease about our future on a national and global level. There is a collective pain that many people don't know what to do with. Some people want to bury their heads in the sand, others don't have that option, and many are looking for ways to cope and even contribute to making things better.

This is a time when we might finally choose to use our collective pain to transform us. We all have a different role to play, and we need to figure out how to work together to make the world a better place for all beings. I believe that as a global culture we are being asked to love bigger than we ever have and that this is what will help us navigate our way out of this overwhelm.

In this chapter I'll begin to touch into what it means to be a global citizen and help build a culture of care for all living things. This requires us to have what I like to call a "global heart." Some questions I ask myself are: How can I turn my overwhelm into overwhelming love? How can I let the whole world into my heart, so my heart can be bigger and more loving? How can I let my heart break open rather than break apart? How can I let my pain transform me? I don't have lots of clear answers to these questions, but I try and let them guide me whenever possible.

"It's All in Our Face Now"

Yesterday, a friend said this to me: "Everything is in our face now. We *can't* get away from all that is happening in the world." Why is it all in our face now? It's partly due to the twenty-four-hour news cycle and our ability to access information about local and global issues with a single click. We receive information (and misinformation and disinformation) at a rate and speed that was unfathomable to the generations before us. None of us can keep up! Our nervous systems were not designed for this amount of input.

I've already discussed the interpersonal impact of technology and social media; there are also political and cultural implications to this technology. On a positive note, social media platforms can spread the stories and messages of those who have been historically silenced. Whether it's a Black mother who lost her child to racially motivated violence or an Indigenous group protecting their land and water, we can connect visually and emotionally to people and events in a way that wasn't possible in the past. With the Internet we can have immediate access to video footage of a school right after a mass shooting and displaced people fleeing violence in other countries. We can donate money, sign petitions, and share their stories to bring awareness to their plight. Social media can be a way to organize movements and protests, such as in Hong Kong or Beirut. Our hyperconnectivity can allow us to be aware of and act swiftly to address some of the tragedies that are happening far away or close by. The author and organizer adrienne maree brown said in a tweet, "Things are not getting worse, they are being revealed. We must hold each other tight and continue to pull back the veil."[1] I agree wholeheartedly, and I think that much of our work as a global society is to face what needs to change while finding ways to unite around a common goal.

Collective Overwhelm

The flip side to all this access is overwhelm. Overwhelm can lead to immobility, apathy, or desensitization. News and information is available to us all day and night, often via notifications on our phones alerting us to breaking news just minutes after an event occurs. This can distract us in moments when we need to be focused on other things, and it can disrupt moments of peace and stillness. A recent study found that the average person in the US checks their phone eighty times a day, and most of us don't go more than ten minutes without looking at our device.[2]

The Center for Humane Technology has a website with ideas for how to control your technology rather than having it control you. The center warns, "The extractive attention economy is tearing apart our shared social fabric."[3] The more that our devices get our attention, the less the world immediately around us does. Many of us are being desensitized as we are overexposed to "breaking news" and shocking headlines multiple times a day.

How often do you find yourself skimming a headline about something that, in the past, would have made you pause, reflect, get more information, or take action? Now we can read something important and just move on to the next thing automatically.

REFLECTION

What are your habits around technology and news?

MEDIA HYGIENE PRACTICE

What can you do to curate your media consumption so that it is deliberate and useful, rather than distracting and overwhelming? Consider how you can set alerts, how you can create time boundaries around technology, and how you can start and end your day.

If you currently stay away from the news completely, what might it look like to engage in a way that is not overwhelming?

In addition to having access to important stories that need to be told, we are inundated with fake news stories curated to enrage and divide us. Often, we don't know what to believe because many news outlets are no longer impartial conveyers of information. They have to compete with the abundance of content available to people, and the only way to get peoples' attention is through sensationalized headlines and stories. In addition, most smartphones and news and entertainment platforms are designed to get us hooked. As James Williams, cofounder of the initiative Time Well Spent, a movement to help people take control of their technology use, says, "The attention economy incentivizes the design of technologies that grab our attention. In so doing, it privileges our impulses over our intentions. That means privileging what is sensational over what is nuanced, appealing to emotion, anger and outrage."[4]

The way that computer algorithms are set up, many of us find ourselves in an echo chamber where we only see the news that is in alignment with our views. Our browsers automatically show us articles that fit our profile and user history. We rarely see opposing points of view, so we get more and more entrenched in what we believe and less exposed to other perspectives. This, coupled with the lack of nuance in most stories, decreases our tolerance of opposing viewpoints. In his book *Why We're Polarized*, Ezra Klein, cofounder of Vox, makes the point that the United States is more politically polarized than ever.[5] Historically, the country's political parties did not generate a strong sense of group affiliation. Each party included people of many races, genders, and economic classes. This is not true today, and people's party affiliation seems to define them more than ever. According to the Pew Research Center, "Political polarization—the vast and growing gap between liberals and conservatives, Republicans and Democrats—is a defining feature of American politics today."[6]

This polarization has us fearing those on the "other side" and pointing fingers at all the ways everyone else is wrong, bad, and even dangerous. We are also fighting among each other and unable to tolerate differences even with people who share our same general viewpoint!

Collective anxiety is running high as people are getting more and more suspicious. Our faith in each other is eroding. We dehumanize people or groups who we perceive don't have the same values as us, and this makes a constructive conversation almost impossible. This is the collective fight-or-flight response in action, and it goes against our best interests. One way to address this collective overwhelm is to challenge this response.

A Paradigm Shift: Collective Care

A culture of collective care asks us to let the whole world into our hearts. To move *toward* one another when things are difficult rather than away. It asks us to see ourselves in everyone, and all people as equal. It asks us to know our different roles in the movement for change and value and respect all roles, even (or perhaps especially) the less visible ones. It requires some of us to step up and some of us to get out of the way. Collective care means that we have each other's backs and think about the impact of our actions on all beings. It invites us to see well-being as everyone's birthright, and our mutual responsibility in ensuring this well-being for everyone as a natural part of life rather than a burden or a form of special altruism.

Addressing our collective anxiety is going to require continued work on many levels—politics, environmental policy, economic structures, education, health care, immigration, and more. One thing we all can do to contribute to a culture of care is redefine what we think well-being is. Kerri Kelly, founder of CTZNWELL,[7] an organization dedicated to democratizing well-being and making it accessible to everyone, says, "Well-being is not a privilege, it is a human right. But we live in a system that privileges well-being to those with time, access, and money. We have a responsibility as citizens to actively create the conditions of belonging, safety, and well-being so that everyone can thrive."[8] A culture of care prioritizes the well-being of all people equally, and it values environmental sustainability and respect for nonhuman life as well. Martin Luther King Jr. called this the Beloved Community, which is a community founded on economic and social justice. When we can participate in a way that contributes toward collective care, we are able to be well ourselves. For some of us, this is exactly the missing element in our journey toward being well.

Practicing collective care is a paradigm shift for those of us brought up in more individualistic cultures. It asks us to reimagine what we have been taught about basic things like who we are, what real happiness is, and how we deal with conflict.

Redefining Self: From Consumer to Citizen

Even though an obsession with accumulating wealth and goods is not a recent occurrence in human history, the shaping of our identity around the accumulation of things and the prioritization of this accumulation has grown dramatically in the past hundred years, especially in industrialized countries. Our well-being has become linked to what we can have rather than who we are being. A fascinating documentary series called *The Century of the Self* traces the history of how Sigmund Freud's nephew, Edward Bernays, used the principles of psychology to help marketers in the United States sell their products. Tim Adams of *The Guardian* writes, "Bernays was among the first to understand that one of the implications of the subconscious mind was that it could be appealed to in order to sell products and ideas. You no longer had to offer people what they needed; by linking your brand with their deeper hopes and fears, you could persuade them to buy what they dreamt of. Equipped with our subconscious wish-lists, we could go shopping for the life we had seen portrayed in the adverts."[9] Getting people to link buying something with feeling good was a very deliberate strategy that continues today. Advertisers shape our ideals and then sell us products that promise to meet these ideals. Whether it's a cream that promises to reduce wrinkles (even though wrinkles are a natural effect of aging), a diet plan that will get rid of fat (even though there is evidence that we can be healthy at any size), or a fancy car that is fast, how many of us are trying to buy our way into an ideal life constructed for us by marketers?

Those of us who live in the US have also been sold this idea that when we buy things we help our country by stimulating economic growth. Yet seeing ourselves as consumers benefits corporations, not us. Even those of us committed to sustainable living who can afford to purchase things made with care can get caught up in our own version of materialism. We may be pining for the electric car rather than the sports car, or the juicer rather than the diet pills, but we still can get overly caught up in consumption, even if it's "conscious."

For all of us in the industrialized world, who consume most of the world's resources and create a disproportionate amount of the world's pollution, our work is to buy less stuff. Period. This can only truly happen when we challenge our values and priorities. When we get totally honest, how much of our energy and attention goes toward accumulating things? Even if we see those things as righteous, can we shift our thoughts away from how we can be more materially comfortable or fashionable toward how we might participate more fully in our community? Also, how do we expand the idea of citizenship beyond our national borders into being a citizen of the world?

REFLECTION

What are your most important values? Where in your life are you living by these values and where can you make some changes?

Redefining Happiness: From Affluenza to Eudaemonia

When we buy into the idea that material things are the source of our happiness, whether we have access to these things or not, we can become afflicted with the malaise of affluenza. Merriam-

Webster defines affluenza as "the unhealthy and unwelcome psychological and social effects of affluence regarded especially as a widespread societal problem: such as feelings of guilt, lack of motivation, and social isolation experienced by wealthy people [and] extreme materialism and consumerism associated with the pursuit of wealth and success and resulting in a life of chronic dissatisfaction, debt, overwork, stress, and impaired relationships."

Individualism and consumerism bolster this false paradigm of happiness, which keeps us in a constant search for things that only give us the illusion of happiness. A paradigm that keeps us all competing with each other in search of the next shiny thing harms everyone. We end up distracted and disillusioned, chasing something that, at the end of the day, is meaningless. Research shows that once we have our basic needs met, having more is not correlated with increased happiness at all.[10]

One element of the collective care paradigm is the concept that our well-being and happiness are linked to each other. We can't be truly well until everyone is well, or at least until everyone has the chance to be well. If we know, even unconsciously, that our happiness comes at the expense of others' well-being, or that while we are enjoying a delicious and satisfying meal so many go hungry, it takes a certain amount of dissociation and denial to move through the world. True happiness must go beyond self-gratification and connect to something bigger. Aristotle described this as "eudaemonia." He saw virtue as part of happiness. There has been a good amount of research that shows that we get more happiness from giving than from receiving. But this goes beyond giving to the less fortunate—it's about living a life dedicated to making sure there's no such thing as "the less fortunate." It's about living a life dedicated to collective liberation from oppression.

Liberation Psychology

Liberation theology is a religious movement that arose in mid-twentieth-century Catholicism that sought to apply religious faith by aiding the poor and oppressed through involvement in political and civic affairs. There are now liberation theologies around the world that center justice for those who are discarded and oppressed by society as a central focus of religion. In contrast to charity, which is about giving to those in need, justice asks us to challenge the conditions that cause so many to be in need to begin with. Liberation psychology, a field that came out of Latin America in the 1970s and was shaped by the values of liberation theology, emerged as a social science that aimed to recognize and address social inequity as a barrier to well-being for oppressed groups. It has since evolved to refer to a social science that sees that inequality hurts everyone, even those who benefit from it. In their book on liberation psychology, my teachers Mary Watkins and Helene Shulman write, "Liberation psychologies understand that the health of individuals and the health of communities, the health of those who suffer from oppression and those who inflict it—categories which sometimes overlap in our complex world—are inextricably intertwined."[11] When we are complicit in the harm of others, whether we are aware of it or not, it undermines our own humanity, our own capacity to be whole. This is because we can't be truly well until everyone is well. Maybe our anxiety is alerting us to this!

In contrast to liberation psychology, traditional Western psychology (which has aimed to follow a medical model of assessing and analyzing the human mind) sees people as discrete entities and locates psychological challenges in the individual—decontextualized and dehistoricized. This model also tells us that we have to "fix" ourselves—heal our anxiety and pain—before we can enter into society in a meaningful way. This way of thinking can exacerbate our anxiety because now our anxiety is also a source of shame and separation from others. Liberation psychology sees all of us as part of a tapestry of life where we are held in community, supporting one another and including one another—not once we're "fixed," but while we are in the process of healing. As I've pointed out before, none of us alive today created systems of inequality, but it is up to all of us to figure out how to change them. Liberation is about healing together, in community. As Watkins and Shulman say, "The question for liberation psychologies is how to create the kinds of environments that enlarge possibilities for aliveness."[12] Practicing liberation requires us to embody, in everything we do, the values we wish to see in the world. This requires us to practice accountability, treat others with dignity, and deal with conflict consciously.

Accountability

When thinking about how to make the world a better place, I know I am guilty of blaming all "those people" out there for the ills of the world. Pointing out what others are doing poorly lets me feel good about myself and superior to everyone else. It also lets me off the hook from changing my own behavior. Practicing accountability is a cornerstone of liberation. Accountability has to do with taking responsibility for our words and actions when we cause harm, taking the steps necessary to repair the relationships involved, and changing our behavior so that we do better going forward. Mia Mingus, a transformative justice and disability justice community organizer, asks, "What if our own accountability wasn't something we ran from, but something we ran towards and desired, appreciated, held as sacred? What if we cherished opportunities to take accountability as precious opportunities to practice liberation? To practice love?"[13]

Having a global heart means seeing taking accountability for our actions as an act of love and solidarity. It allows us to be flawed and maintain connection and trust. It also frees up all the energy many of us use defending ourselves, denying our behavior, or hiding from each other. Accountability is an attitude of self-responsibility rooted in a healthy sense of culpability and self-examination. Accountability is not about shame. Shame is immobilizing; accountability is generative. It is rooted in dignity for ourselves and for others.

Restoring Dignity

Donna Hicks, author of *Dignity: Its Essential Role in Resolving Conflict*, talks about threats to people's dignity being a major cause of conflict and violence around the world. She has come to this conclusion after years of doing international conflict resolution work. Hicks distinguishes dignity from respect. The latter must be earned, but dignity is a birthright. "We must treat others as if they matter, as if they are worthy of care and attention. This must be the baseline for all our interactions."[14] As you read this, it might resonate and make sense. But imagine being asked to do this with someone who has harmed you, or someone who would harm you if they could, or holds beliefs that you strongly disagree with. Notice what happens in your body as you picture this. It's likely you may first feel some sort of fight, flight, or freeze response.

Conflict can bring up our instinct to protect ourselves and shut away the source of the perceived danger or discomfort. A paradigm of collective care asks us to maintain a baseline of dignity in *all* our interactions. It asks us to move away from a self-preservation impulse to one of self-extension. Threats to our dignity bring up primitive responses that feel like a threat to our life. Hicks says we have to tap into our capacity to self-reflect as part of making this shift. This is what the first part of this book is focused on—helping us cultivate our ability for self-reflection and self-regulation. This can help us extend our sense of self beyond our own individual interests.

Kazu Haga, activist and author of *Healing Resistance*, says, "The best way to protect those that we love is to love those that may hurt them." He reminds us that only those that have lost touch with their own humanity have the capacity to perpetrate harm on others deliberately. We must have compassion for them and stand for the restoration of their humanity and dignity if we want to truly find peace. When we do this, it can also reduce our own pain and suffering. We see this in the story of Mary Johnson and Oshea Israel. Oshea murdered Mary's son, Laramiun Byrd, during a conflict when he was a teenager. Mary wished that Oshea would have gotten more than fifteen years for murdering her only child. She saw Oshea as an animal; she hated him. Mary talks about how the hate that festered in her for the years after her son's death turned to a deep-seated bitterness that pushed everyone away from her. Oshea shares that he pushed down his guilt and shame and maintained a story about his victim that justified his behavior. This caused him his own version of pain and suffering. When the two finally met, both expressed the relief of seeing the humanity of the other—Mary saw Oshea's pain and remorse, and Oshea stopped denying the humanity of the person he killed. Both were freed of their pain when the dignity of the other was restored, and true forgiveness happened. They found peace.

REFLECTION

Where in your life are you dealing with conflict by separating and defending? Where are you holding a grudge and unable the see the humanity in the person you're struggling with? What could be possible if you kept that person's dignity intact in how you approached the conflict?

RESTORING DIGNITY LETTER-WRITING PRACTICE

Pick one or two of the situations you identified above. Then write three letters to that person (or people) that you do not necessarily plan to send.

Letter 1: Fully express your anger, rage, or disappointment without editing yourself. Allow yourself to blame and shame, whatever you feel. Get all your most primal feelings out, unedited. (Do *not* send this letter!)

Letter 2: Write a letter using only "I" statements. Express how you feel, share your own experience of this situation or dynamic (e.g., "I felt disappointed/sad/confused when . . ."). If you find yourself starting to blame the other person, put those statements in letter 1.

Letter 3: This last letter should be written with the intention of trying to understand the other person's experience. This letter is an attempt to be curious and explore how their behavior might be a product of their own trauma or threat to their dignity. You might write things like, "I'm wondering what you were feeling when . . ." or, "I imagine you were in a lot of pain when . . . ." You may need to use your somatic tools here to stay regulated. If you feel overwhelmed, take a break and come back to this another time.

Conflict Transformation

When dignity is the baseline, conflict can be an opportunity for both parties to be transformed and even healed. This is true from minor conflicts to even the most atrocious acts of violence such as murder or rape. John Paul Lederach, author of *The Little Book of Conflict Transformation*, says that "conflict . . . creates life: through conflict we respond, innovate and change."[15] We live in a culture that generally doesn't deal well with conflict. We see it as something to be avoided. When it comes to the US criminal justice system, conflict is dealt with by punishing the perpetrator. Even if rehabilitative services are offered, there is almost never a chance for victims and perpetrators to engage with each other. In contrast, the model of restorative justice is one where justice is not in the hands of the state or the police but the community. This model invites perpetrators, victims, and all stakeholders to decide collectively what justice is and how to hold perpetrators accountable. Sometimes this means involving the criminal justice system and sometimes it doesn't.

The current system, which sends a perpetrator to prison, for example, and doesn't allow any contact with the victim, makes no room for relational resolution and healing. Some victims may feel good knowing their perpetrator is locked away. The idea of seeing them is traumatic and may not be useful. But for some, the separation maintains a disconnect between the two parties whereby neither person has to confront the humanity of the other. Sometimes it can be in seeing each other's humanity that they can begin to let go of the pain they carry. When we dehumanize someone else, it costs us our own humanity. No one wins.

The story of Ian Manuel (which you can read in full in Bryan Stevenson's book *Just Mercy*) is a powerful one. When he was thirteen years old, Ian shot a woman, Debbie Berkovitz, during a botched robbery. She survived, and Ian was sentenced to life without parole. He was the youngest person ever to receive such a sentence, and he spent almost eighteen years in solitary confinement because he was too young to be housed with the adult prison population. Ian called Debbie during one of his permitted calls and apologized for what he did. They began speaking regularly and got to know one another. Eventually Debbie began to have compassion for young Ian and forgave him for shooting her. She ended up petitioning the courts herself, claiming that Ian's sentence was too harsh. After twenty-six years, he was released thanks to the help of Debbie and the Equal Justice Initiative. Today Ian is an inspirational speaker and advocate, dedicating his life to spreading a message of peace, love, and justice. It is a beautiful story of the healing that can happen when people are able to see each other's humanity despite violence and conflict.

The nonprofit organization Healing Dialogue and Action has brought together hundreds of victims and perpetrators, like Ian and Debbie, to dialogue and find peace with each other.[16] Throughout the restorative justice process, both parties are coached and supported in advance of the meeting in order to show up in the most constructive way. It can take years of preparation; the process usually consists of lots of self-reflection and accountability work, especially for the perpetrator. Some of the dialogues have been captured on film; seeing the interaction is a powerful testament to our capacity to heal together. Often the two parties show up nervous and hesitant. In a successful dialogue, the victim shares the impact of the perpetrator's actions on their life and the perpetrator shares their story and takes responsibility for their actions, which are usually rooted in pain and trauma. The victim or victim's loved ones are able to witness the humanity in the perpetrator. Even if the victim is not able to forgive, they might be able to understand better what brought the other person to do what they did. When successful, the dialogue is healing for both parties and allows for a resolution beyond what the criminal justice system can bring.

REFLECTION

What is your general attitude about conflict with others? Are you willing to consider that some of these conflicts can have the potential to transform all parties if they are addressed with that intention in mind? How might your views on personal conflict extend to the ways our broader systems, such as the criminal justice system, the educational system, or the political system, approach conflict?

GLOBAL HEART REFLECTION

What does the "global heart" mean to you? How might this concept help you alleviate your anxiety or pain? Write your answer in poem form and/or draw it.

10

Self-Reflection and Action

Living a Life Oriented toward What Is Possible

AT THE BEGINNING of this book, I told you that I would take you on a journey from individual well-being to collective liberation. So, what is collective liberation? The term is often credited to bell hooks and her essay "Love as the Practice of Freedom." It describes a state of freedom founded on not participating in systems of domination but rather coming from an ethic of love. This is a state where no one is stepped on so others can thrive. Collective liberation is both a way of life and a vision of a future where there is truly justice and equity for all beings. A future where everyone has the possibility to thrive.

In chapter 7, I talked about the notion of expanding our circle of compassion. When we extend our care beyond ourselves, it's hard to be truly happy if our own personal needs are met but we are not contributing in any way to making sure everyone else can have their basic needs met. We recognize that our liberation is bound, and that true well-being requires a world where everyone can be well. There's an idea that I find true as a parent, which is that you are only as happy as your least happy child. Imagine a world where we could hold the suffering of the most vulnerable in our heart all the time—not in a way that would be overwhelming or immobilizing, but in a way that guided all of our actions and values. I'm not suggesting we need to be martyrs; I'm suggesting that our pursuit of happiness has to come with a pursuit of justice—otherwise, it's empty.

Critical consciousness is a term coined by Paulo Freire, a Brazilian educator and philosopher who was an advocate of using education as a tool for liberation. Critical consciousness is about developing an awareness of yourself that includes the sociopolitical context you are in. According to this framework, it's not enough to be conscious of certain parts of ourselves, such as our personal and familial history, for example, without also being conscious of other things that shape who we are, such as our race, class, gender, ability, sexuality, religion, ancestry, and so forth. Xochitl Frausto, a queer Xicanx author and organizer, says: "Love yourself. But also analyze and be critical of how you think, act, and behave. Self-love without self-awareness is useless. Be accountable." Critical consciousness is about accountability; it includes an action component because cultivating this type of awareness should spur us to act in order to push back against the broader dynamics that are harmful to so many. For some of us, finding ways to act aimed at shifting these broader issues can help channel our anxiety into productive and life-affirming actions and ways of being. Addressing what might be underlying our suffering beyond our personal or interpersonal interests is what critical consciousness is about.

Sometimes I remind my students that they can't be selectively conscious. This is when we limit our sphere of reflection and awareness to our personal and interpersonal lives. If our aware-ness doesn't include a broader investigation of what is happening socially and politically, it's incomplete. The nonprofit I cofounded, Off the Mat, Into the World, aims to do exactly this: get people to connect their personal practices to how they engage with the world. Some people come to our trainings and actually need to do the reverse—pause from engaging with the world to focus on their personal practice. Often these are activists who have spent so much of their time addressing the broader, systemic problems in the world that they lose connection with themselves and their own humanity. Some of them burn out and some of them end up replicating the dynamics that they are fighting against in the world in their personal lives. They are needing to come back to themselves and do the personal work it takes to continue their good work in a sustainable and effective way. In finding peace from our anxiety, it can be helpful to notice which side of this spectrum we're on—supporting the world but not ourselves, or focused on ourselves but not the world—and try to find a way to achieve balance between the two.

In my own journey of self-discovery, I spent a lot of time focusing on things that I thought were the most impactful in shaping me—my personal traumas, my relationship with my family, my gender, my personality and temperament. For a long time, I thought these were the most significant factors that shaped my identity and how I moved through the world. I spent over a decade exploring various aspects of myself, trying to make sense of who I was. I did lots of personal therapy, group therapy, movement practices like yoga and dance, meditation, and self-reflection. These factors were indeed important in my life, but after a while I got stuck in a somewhat narcissistic bubble of self-examination and self-reflection. It preoccupied me and I got fairly disconnected from events in the rest of the world or any issue that did not directly impact me or my immediate circle. These things felt like distractions in my quest to know myself. Some of the teachers I came across encouraged disconnection from the larger world in order to truly be a dedicated seeker of "truth." This extreme focus on self-reflection actually made me quite neurotic and self-centered.

When I broadened my view of myself, it forced me to confront things I had never thought of. It was challenging and embarrassing at times, but it also helped me find even more meaning and purpose in my life's choices. I began to understand the role privilege plays in my life, and how I am connected and even accountable to others I don't know in ways I hadn't thought of. My privilege included things like my class background, and the fact that I am neurotypical and my brain works in a way that allows me to meet mainstream education and social standards. I also acknowledged how being thin and fitting into dominant beauty standards gave me an advantage in many areas of my life. Being straight and cisgender meant I never had to feel excluded from dominant narratives about gender and sexuality. As an able-bodied person, buildings are designed for me, and I never have to figure out where the ramps are or if information is available in braille. So much of the world is shaped to accommodate someone like me. I'm even right-handed! I also reflected on the impact of being an immigrant and how so much of my personality was formed by trying to fit in to a culture different from mine.

Realizing all the advantages I've had has also shed light on how so many people don't have all of these advantages that I've always taken for granted. Privilege is often invisible to those who have it. Privilege means there are certain things we don't have to confront, because the world is designed to ease our path in particular ways. When people aren't privileged by the systems around us, they are acutely aware of it. They are more vulnerable to the unfair laws and policies of these systems. For example, low-income people don't have access to adequate health care; if they even have health care, the policies are often limited and may not cover necessary medications or treatment. People who use wheelchairs can't count on wheelchair-accessible transit or public spaces. Transgender people may not be able to get matching identity documents. People of color and undocumented people may not feel able to go to the police for help. So many people live in a world that doesn't have their back at all. And some live in a world where they are constant targets.

It's important to note that most of us are privileged in some ways and marginalized in others, and having privilege in some respects doesn't mean you haven't had to face any challenges in your life. Also, just because someone has experienced a great deal of advantage in life doesn't mean they are necessarily happy or at peace. Similarly, many people who do not have many advantages survive and thrive despite their circumstances. They just have more external obstacles to surmount. Critical consciousness should not be used to box people into assumptions about their resilience or capacity or have us competing on who is more oppressed or advantaged. It is simply an awareness of the external circumstances that can shape us. Critical consciousness needs to be cultivated along with self-reflection and self-investigation. It can bring depth and nuance to our sense of self. It also allows us to view others with a broader lens as well.

Developing critical consciousness by exploring how current and historical social and political contexts shape us and those around us can also give us access into greater awareness and empathy for others because we can begin to realize how what we can and can't see is determined by the larger systems that we are a part of. Some of us don't have to see certain things that others are forced to see. Critical consciousness is what allows us to open our hearts to the world. It can allow us to see a fuller picture and thus participate more fully and more authentically.

IDENTITY REFLECTION

On a sheet of paper, create three columns. In the first write down parts of your identity that are privileged by society, in the second write down parts of your identity that are marginalized, unseen, or pathologized by society, and in the third write down parts that are complicated (e.g., privileged in one setting but not another). Think about things like your race, gender, class, education level, citizenship, ability, mental health, cognitive functioning, religion, body size, sexuality, age, and as many other characteristics as you can think of. Take some time to reflect on how the things in each column have impacted your life.

Love Ethic

Critical consciousness can help us love bigger and better than we ever thought we could. It can help us see ourselves and each other with more empathy and compassion, which can then allow us to act from a place of mutuality and our shared humanity despite our differences. One idea that guides much of my life choices comes from philosopher, activist, and author Cornel West. He says, "Justice is what love looks like in public." Living a life committed to justice for all is an act of love.[1] In the essay mentioned earlier, "Love as the Practice of Freedom," bell hooks warns us that "without love, our efforts to liberate ourselves and our world community from oppression and exploitation are doomed."[2] She calls for an ethic of love to guide and shape our social and political movements. Love, in other words, is what is needed to guide our actions if we are going to live into the world we want. Activists, scholars, and religious leaders have been calling on centering love in our social movements for generations—from Jesus, Gandhi,

Martin Luther King Jr., and Grace Lee Boggs to leaders in the present-day racial justice movement, disability justice movement, reproductive justice movement, and other liberation movements. By love, they aren't talking about having a warm and fuzzy feeling about everyone; rather, they are talking about what Gandhi called *ahimsa* and King explained as *agape*: a love that is unconditional, that is grounded in goodwill toward all, that recognizes that all life is interconnected and that harming someone else is an act of harming oneself.

An aspen grove is a powerful metaphor for this love grounded in our interdependence. The roots of aspen trees are connected underground, and in order for the system to be strong, all the roots must be healthy. Some trees may be older than others, some may be in shady places or have damaged trunks. Research is showing that trees actually help one another and send nutrients toward the more vulnerable saplings who need it and can't access it themselves. Radical love is rooting for (pun intended) the health of the entire system. Not out of pity or sympathy, but because we know that we are all better off this way.

Imagine that we could aim to see our shared humanity in this way rather than as a hierarchy where some people are valued more and are thus afforded easier access to what they need to survive. Right now, the people and communities that are currently under-resourced by the larger systems have to do more with less. If and when this is true for you, then your self-preservation is what you are contributing to the health of the larger community; it's your expression of love. (The tree that is in the dry part of the grove has to work extra hard to survive; for the health of the system, it needs to focus on taking in nutrients.) However, some people are currently over-resourced by the larger systems. If and when this is true for you, sharing energy and resources with others is not only your contribution to caring for the collective but it can also help heal your anxiety, because, as we've seen, reaching out to offer support is one way to overcome trauma and anxiety. A love ethic means that we heal by caring for one another (collective care) and we understand that sometimes we need to be cared for and sometimes we offer out the care, and one is not better than the other. Our end goal is a world where everyone is valued equally, and the ways we are different are celebrated and supported rather than judged and categorized. This may feel like a daunting vision given the state of the world today. This is where the idea of active hope can be helpful.

Active Hope

In the book *Active Hope*, Joanna Macy and Chris Johnstone define active hope as "identifying the outcomes we hope for and then playing an active role in bringing them about." It means that "we don't wait until we are sure of success."[3] Active hope requires us to honor our pain as an indication of how much we care. When we can stay with the pain, it can motivate us to act, but when we run away from the pain, we also run away from the hope. I had a professor of environmental studies in college who refused to recycle. He felt that the environmental crisis was so big that recycling wasn't going to have a significant impact in the grand scheme of things. Even if he was right, I imagine that each time he put recyclable items in the trash bin it reminded him of his lack of hope. Even if we feel like particular actions are insignificant, they can fuel our commitment to live in a way that moves us in the direction of healing and wholeness.

Active hope is not about denying reality; it's about being grounded in reality while moving toward what we want even if we don't see evidence of it occurring yet. When I'm teaching yoga,

I often invite my students to do this while they are in a stretch. I ask them to feel the tension without denying it, while knowing they are moving toward more flexibility. Active hope asks us to hold pain and possibility at the same time, giving possibility a slight advantage so that we stay motivated to act. The way I see it, even if we are doomed and none of this is going to work, I'd rather live my life in service of a world that is life-affirming. What's the alternative?

Taking Action

There are infinite ways we can participate and contribute to shifting a world where everyone can be well. Joanna Macy calls this the "Great Turning." This refers to a "shift from a self-destroying political economy to one in harmony with the Earth."[4] (This includes people being in harmony with each other of course.) In her framework there are three mutually reinforcing ways we can contribute to this shift: holding actions, structural change, and shift in consciousness. I'll share the basics of these three kinds of work, and I recommend that you check out her book *World as Lover, World as Self* to explore this more deeply.[5]

"Holding actions" are actions to resist or slow the damage and destruction to the Earth and its beings. These include the political, legislative, and legal work required to reduce environmental destruction, as well as direct actions such as blockades, boycotts, and civil disobedience. They can also include the things we do to minimize the pain of those who are negatively impacted, such as serving food at a food bank; contributing time or money to organizations working with vulnerable groups like people living with homelessness, mental health conditions, or addiction; and offering services such as yoga and meditation, education, or skill training to people who are incarcerated. Holding actions can also be things like recycling, intervening if you hear someone acting or speaking in a bigoted way, and buying sustainably and ethically sourced goods.

"Structural change" is about creating alternatives to systems and structures that cause so much harm. This is about understanding how the larger systems that we are a part of operate, including but not limited to economics, law and politics, education, health care, agriculture, and food production. By understanding these structures, we can then design or demand new structures that are better. Developing critical consciousness is part of this, as is work around issues such as prison abolition, alternative education models, and new economic and political models as well as ecological solutions that go beyond dealing with the symptoms of environmental destruction and social inequality and move us toward environmental sustainability, justice, and equity.

The final dimension of this work is "shift in consciousness," which is a paradigm shift in worldview and values. This shift is about realizing our interdependence and our need for sustainability and collective care. Macy says that structural alternatives like the ones above can't succeed without this (I agree!). She says, "Like our ancestors, we begin again to see the world as our body and . . . as sacred."[6] The work and reflection that this book has asked you to do falls into this category. As we connect our individual need for peace from anxiety to a broader need for collective peace, we see that our body (nervous system) is inextricably linked to the larger collective "body." Other ways we can contribute to this shift can include how we raise our children and support the young people in our community, teaching, healing work, writing, or mentoring. Art and music can shift consciousness. Some of the most effective ways we challenge the status quo is through learning new ways of being together that are collaborative, creative, and restorative. Reimagining how we might work together, live together, and collaborate can help shift consciousness and give us an embodied experience of connection and interdependence.

REFLECTION

Are you already contributing to one of these categories in your life, even in small ways? If so, how? What are some actions you can take in your life right now that would contribute to a paradigm of collective care and liberation? Use Macy's categories if you like.

The following is a list created by Tessa Hicks Peterson from her book *Student Development and Social Justice*.[7] Tessa is a professor of cultural studies at Pitzer College, and she runs the community engagement center there. The following things are more tangible actions that are aimed at making a change on a systemic level:

- giving money or time to organizations making change on the ground level
- engaging with a local community or organization to conduct community-based participatory research or service aimed at creating larger structural shifts over time
- calling or writing elected officials to voice support for or protest against specific legislation that impacts equity and justice
- organizing or attending rallies, protests, marches, or teach-ins
- educating yourself about and then voting in public elections for issues you believe in and candidates you think will best represent them
- participating in neighborhood or city councils to push for local change
- creating or attending gatherings in your neighborhood with others seeking to organize grassroots social change efforts

- participating in organizational change within institutions (religious or professional or civic) of which you are a part, including questioning if or how these institutions may be unwittingly colluding in upholding longstanding oppressive structures
- participating in grassroots collaborations that provide alternative community structures or systems
- bearing witness to suffering and raising your voice against it
- recognizing and changing personal biases
- calling others up when unjust or discriminatory comments are made
- engaging in difficult dialogues with people who have different life experiences or beliefs than you do to see if you can build common ground or bridges of understanding
- relearning history from the point of view of the oppressed
- addressing the reproduction of inequalities in your own life (including in your intimate relationships and school or work communities)
- healing yourself and your community from the trauma of injustice

Notice if this list overwhelms you and part of you feels like you should be doing all the things on it. Remember: it's your job to do *your piece* of this work. If everyone did their piece, our world would change radically. When we take on too much or think we should do more than we're capable of, it serves no one. It can lead to burnout and overwhelm. Sometimes we find we can take on one piece directly (e.g., participating in local city council meetings) and support others indirectly (e.g., donating to organizations doing the work you can't do).

REFLECTION

What items on this list are you already doing? What items are things that you might be able to start doing? What is your specific piece of this work toward collective liberation right now?

Conclusion

These are intense times, and feeling the urgency on a personal, interpersonal, and collective level means you're paying attention. If you find yourself creating unrealistic expectations for yourself or the people around you in a way that, ironically, creates more separation or shutdown, revise your standards! Be more forgiving. Whether it's using somatic tools, working on building your connection ecosystem, or developing critical consciousness, chances are your process will be clunky. You'll have moments of feeling the positive impact of this work, and you'll have moments of feeling like an awkward adolescent fumbling through life.

I believe that everyone on this planet wants peace. Peace from anxiety, peace from conflict, and peace from the illusion of separation. I believe that we can all find ways to let our anxiety and suffering open us up to being more compassionate and integrated so that we can contribute to a reality where everything we do is based on recognizing our interdependence. This is not a new idea. Many cultures have a version of this concept in their worldview. The Sanskrit word *namaste*, a respectful greeting commonly used in India, means "I bow to you." This can affirm the notion as we bow to each other that beneath all the ways we are different, we are essentially the same. *Ubuntu*, a Nguni Bantu term, is often translated as "I am because we are." It is about interconnectedness and the idea that no individual can exist without the community and no community is whole without all of its members. Many Indigenous cultures have ideologies rooted in collective care and deep connection. The Lakota phrase *Aho Mitakuye Oyasin* reflects the Lakota value of centering right relationship in all that we do. The Cree word *wahkohtowin* means "everything is related" and is one of the basic principles of Cree Natural Law, which is meant to keep individuals, communities, and societies healthier.

Mainstream culture teaches us that our anxiety is an individual problem with individual causes; this is part of the problem. Hopefully this book has illuminated how collective anxiety requires collective healing and liberation. I think this work is a process of re-membering (the opposite of dis-membering)— calling in the lost parts of ourselves individually and collectively, remembering our deepest connections and the vital role each of us plays in this web of life. As we begin to see our anxiety as a call for healing, we can allow it to transform all of us. This requires us to find new ways of being together so that everyone is honored and included exactly as they are. So, let's be willing to practice these new ways of being together where we center our shared humanity as we work toward building a world where everyone has the chance to be well and thrive.

ACKNOWLEDGMENTS

I DID NOT write this book alone. Even though I spent hundreds of hours at my keyboard alone, I would never have had the time and space to write if it weren't for the people who helped me by caring for my kids, making meals, and taking on work tasks for me. Thank you to my amazing husband, Paul Eckstein, not just for your unwavering faith in me and support but for allowing me to tell parts of our story. To my sisters Lara and Kristine, and my mom, Dalal, who didn't live to see the publication of this book but was there when it was birthed: you always have my back and it means more than you'll ever know. To my children, Sebastian and Marley: you are my inspiration. I dedicate my life to leaving this world a better place for you and the next generations. Thank you Julia—you were with us in the last few months of writing, making sure I had time and space to write in the midst of the pandemic quarantine and such chaotic times on our planet.

I want to thank all of you who took time to read parts of the book and give me your feedback. I asked you because I trust you to be honest and hold me accountable: Seane Corn, Suzanne Sterling, Laura Sharkey, Ginny Smith, Felina Dalanis, Teo Drake, Jacoby Ballard, Carol Horton, and Tessa Hicks Peterson. To Alex Kapitan (www.radicalcopyeditor.com), knowing you had your eye on every word allows me to publish this book with a confidence I would never have had without you. Thank you to my Shambhala editors, Sarah Stanton and Breanna Locke, for your support and confidence in me and my writing.

Thank you to Seane Corn, Suzanne Sterling, Anita Akhavan, and the whole Off the Mat faculty and staff. My work has grown and matured because of my collaboration with you and our work together that I am so proud of. I am so grateful to Peter Levine and my training in Somatic Experiencing, which laid the foundation for my understanding of trauma and resilience. I'm also grateful for my work with A Thousand Joys—Liza Auciello, Victoria Alvarado and Hillary Johnson—I was able to grow my work with the opportunities you gave me to bring it to educators and mental health professionals. I have so much gratitude for my teachers at Pacifica Graduate Institute who helped me decolonize my mind and think about healing in a holistic and critical way.

Finally, I want to thank all the students and clients I've worked with over the past twenty years who trusted me enough to share their deepest stories with me. You are all my teachers. I'm honored to have walked this path with you in some way or another. I hold all of you in my heart, and I do this work so we can all be well together.

NOTES

Introduction: Anxiety and These Overwhelming Times

1. "Facts & Statistics," Anxiety and Depression Association of America, accessed August 7, 2020, https://adaa.org/about-adaa/press-room/facts -statistics.
2. Matthew Taylor and Jessica Murray, "'Overwhelming and Terrifying': The Rise of Climate Anxiety," *The Guardian*, February 10, 2020, www.theguardian.com/environment/2020/feb/10/overwhelming-and -terrifying-impact-of-climate-crisis-on-mental-health.

Chapter 1. Your Body Is Your GPS

1. Mihaly Csikszentmihalyi, *Flow: The Psychology of Optimal Experience* (New York: Harper Row, 2009).
2. Eberhard Fuchs and Gabriele Flügge, "Adult Neuroplasticity: More Than 40 Years of Research," *Hindawi*, May 4, 2014, www.hindawi .com/journals/np/2014/541870/.
3. Nancy K. Dess, "Tend and Befriend," *Psychology Today*, September 1, 2000, www.psychologytoday.com/us/articles/200009/tend-and-befriend.
4. Mark D. Seery, E. Alison Holman, and Roxane Cohen Silver, "Whatever Does Not Kill Us: Cumulative Lifetime Adversity, Vulnerability, and Resilience," *Journal of Personality and Social Psychology* 99, no. 6 (2010): 1025–41, https://doi.org/10.1037/a0021344.

5. Kelly McGonigal, *The Upside of Stress: Why Stress Is Good for You, and How to Get Good at It* (New York: Avery, 2016).

6. Mark Epstein, *The Trauma of Everyday Life* (New York: Penguin Books, 2014).

7. Peter A. Levine, *Waking the Tiger: Healing Trauma: The Innate Capacity to Transform Overwhelming Experiences* (Berkeley, CA: North Atlantic Books, 1997).

8. C Holden, "Paul MacLean and the Triune Brain," *Science* 204, no. 4397 (August 1979): 1066–68, https://doi.org/10.1126/science.377485.

9. Image inspired by and adapted from Foundation for Human Enrichment.

Chapter 2. Trusting Your Body Again

1. Jalāl al-Dīn Rūmī and Coleman Barks, *The Essential Rumi: New Expanded Edition* (San Francisco: Harper, 2004).

2. Rick Hanson and Richard Mendius, *Buddha's Brain: The Practical Neuroscience of Happiness, Love, and Wisdom* (Oakland, CA: New Harbinger Publications, 2009).

3. Joy DeGruy Leary and Randall Robinson, *Post Traumatic Slave Syndrome: America's Legacy of Enduring Injury and Healing* (Portland, OR: Joy DeGruy Publications Inc., 2018).

4. Rachel Yehuda and Amy Lehrner, "Intergenerational Transmission of Trauma Effects: Putative Role of Epigenetic Mechanisms," *World Psychiatry* 17, no. 3 (2018): 243–57, https://doi.org/10.1002/wps.20568.

5. Bessel A. van der Kolk, *The Body Keeps the Score: Brain, Mind, and Body in the Healing of Trauma* (New York: Penguin, 2015), 17.

Chapter 3. Reclaiming Our Capacity to Heal

1. Ayako Sugawara et al., "Effects of Interoceptive Training on Decision Making, Anxiety, and Somatic Symptoms," *BioPsychoSocial Medicine* 14, no. 7 (March 2020), doi:10.1186/s13030-020-00179-7.

2. Antoine Bechara et al., "Insensitivity to Future Consequences Following Damage to Human Prefrontal Cortex," *Cognition* 50, no. 1–3 (1994): 7–15, https://doi.org/10.1016/0010-0277(94)90018-3.

3. Brené Brown, *Dare to Lead: Brave Work. Tough Conversations. Whole Hearts.* (New York: Random House, 2018), 85.

4. Jonathan Mooney, *Normal Sucks: How to Live, Learn, and Thrive Outside the Lines* (New York: Henry Holt and Company, 2019).

5. "SE Trauma Institute Practitioner Directory," SETI Practitioner Directory, Somatic Experiencing Trauma Institute, accessed August 7, 2020, https://directory.traumahealing.org.

6. Audre Lorde, *A Burst of Light: And Other Essays* (Mineola, New York: Ixia Press, 2017), 130.

Chapter 4. Transforming Trauma

1. Peter A. Levine, *Waking the Tiger: Healing Trauma; The Innate Capacity to Transform Overwhelming Experiences* (Berkeley, CA: North Atlantic Books, 1997), 2.

2. D. W. Winnicott, T. Berry Brazelton, Stanley I. Greenspan, and Benjamin Spock, *Winnicott on the Child* (Cambridge, MA: Perseus, 2002).

3. Michael Marshall, "US Police Kill Up to 6 Times More Black People than White People," *New Scientist*, June 24, 2020, www.newscientist .com/article/2246987-us-police-kill-up-to-6-times-more-black-people -than-white-people/.

4. Christopher Ingraham, "How Rising Inequality Hurts Everyone, Even the Rich," *Washington Post*, February 6, 2018, www.washington post.com/news/wonk/wp/2018/02/06/how-rising-inequality-hurts -everyone-even-the-rich/.

5. Jonathan Haidt, *The Happiness Hypothesis: Finding Modern Truth in Ancient Wisdom* (New York: Basic Books, 2006), 136.

6. Ibid.

7. Please note that I am intentionally using the terms "disabled people" and "autistics" because that's the language that Laura and many other

autistic and/or disabled people prefer. I use the terms "people with disabilities" and "disabled people" interchangeably for this reason. For more information on person-centered language, check out this article by Radical Copyeditor Alex Kapitan: "On 'Person-First Language': It's Time to Actually Put the Person First," Radical Copyeditor, July 13, 2018, https://radicalcopyeditor.com/2017/07/03/person-centered -language.

8. Eli Clare, *Brilliant Imperfection: Grappling with Cure* (Durham: Duke University Press, 2017).

Chapter 5. A Few Thoughts about Suffering

1. Krista Tippet, *On Being*, podcast, January 2020.
2. Desmond Tutu, Dalai Lama, and Douglas Abrams, *The Book of Joy: Lasting Happiness in a Changing World* (New York: Avery, 2016), 7.
3. Teo Drake, "Vibrancy on the Margins: AIDS, Solidarity, and Justice," Roots Grow the Tree, June 11, 2018, https://rootsgrowthetree.com /2015/12/02/vibrancy-on-the-margins.
4. Thich Nhat Hanh, "The Fourteen Precepts of Engaged Buddhism," *Lion's Roar*, April 12, 2017, www.lionsroar.com/the-fourteen-precepts -of-engaged-buddhism/.
5. Pema Chödrön, "How to Practice Tonglen," *Lion's Roar*, May 20, 2020. www.lionsroar.com/how-to-practice-tonglen.

Chapter 6. Connection Is the Key

1. Sharon Salzberg, *Lovingkindness: The Revolutionary Art of Happiness* (Boston: Shambhala, 1995), 1.
2. Harry Harlow, "The Nature of Love," *American Psychologist* 13, no. 12 (1958): 673–85. doi:10.1037/h0047884.
3. Bessel A. van der Kolk, *The Body Keeps the Score: Brain, Mind, and Body in the Healing of Trauma* (New York: Penguin, 2015), 79.
4. Julianne Holt-Lunstad, "The Potential Public Health Relevance of Social Isolation and Loneliness: Prevalence, Epidemiology, and Risk

Factors," *Public Policy and Aging Report* 27, no. 4 (2017): 127–30, https://doi.org/10.1093/ppar/prx030.

5. Shainna Ali, "What You Need to Know about the Loneliness Epidemic," *Psychology Today,* July 12, 2018, www.psychologytoday .com/us/blog/modern-mentality/201807/what-you-need-know-about -the-loneliness-epidemic.

6. Ibid.

7. John T. Cacioppo and William Patrick, *Loneliness: Human Nature and the Need for Social Connection* (New York: W. W. Norton & Company, 2008).

8. Jack Kornfield, *After the Ecstasy, the Laundry: How the Heart Grows Wise on the Spiritual Path* (New York: Bantam Books, 2001), xiii.

9. Johann Hari, "Everything You Think You Know about Addiction Is Wrong," *TED*, 2015, www.ted.com/talks/johann_hari_everything _you_think_you_know_about_addiction_is_wrong.

10. Naina Bajekal, "Want to Win the War on Drugs? Portugal Might Have the Answer," *Time*, August 1, 2018, https://time.com/longform /portugal-drug-use-decriminalization.

11. Bruce K. Alexander, "Addiction: The Urgent Need for a Paradigm Shift," *Substance Use and Misuse* 47, no. 13–14 (2012): 1475–82, https://doi.org/10.3109/10826084.2012.705681.

12. Kelly McGonigal, *The Upside of Stress: Why Stress Is Good for You, and How to Get Good at It* (New York: Avery, 2016), 135–80.

13. Tristen K. Inagaki and Naomi I. Eisenberger, "Neural Correlates of Giving Support to a Loved One," *Psychosomatic Medicine* 74, no. 1 (2012): 3–7, https://doi.org/10.1097/psy.0b013e3182359335.

14. Ervin Staub and Johanna Vollhardt, "Altruism Born of Suffering: The Roots of Caring and Helping after Victimization and Other Trauma," *American Journal of Orthopsychiatry* 78, no. 3 (2008): 267– 80, https://doi.org/10.1037/a0014223.

15. Thomas Constantine Maroukis, *Peyote and the Yankton Sioux: The Life and Times of Sam Necklace* (Oklahoma: University of Oklahoma Press, 2005), 190.

Chapter 7. Creating a Connection Ecosystem

1. Jason G. Goldman, "Ed Tronick and the 'Still Face Experiment,'" *Scientific American*, October 18, 2010, https://blogs.scientificamerican .com/thoughtful-animal/ed-tronick-and-the-8220-still-face-experi ment-8221.

2. Harville Hendrix, *Getting the Love You Want: A Guide for Couples* (New York: Perennial Library, 1990).

3. "Cigna Takes Action to Combat the Rise of Loneliness and Improve Mental Wellness in America," Cigna, January 23, 2020, www.cigna .com/newsroom/news-releases/2020/cigna-takes-action-to-combat -the-rise-of-loneliness-and-improve-mental-wellness-in-america.

4. Cal Newport, *Digital Minimalism: Choosing a Focused Life in a Noisy World* (New York: Portfolio, 2019), 93.

Chapter 8. Connecting with Something Bigger

1. Julian Walker Yoga, website, accessed August 7, 2020, https://julian walkeryoga.com.

2. Andy Fisher, *Radical Ecopsychology: Psychology in the Service of Life* (Albany: State University of New York Press, 2013), 190.

3. Warren Grossman, *To Be Healed by the Earth* (New York: Seven Stories, 2007).

4. Suzanne Sterling, website, accessed August 7, 2020, www.suzanne sterling.com.

Chapter 9. The Global Heart

1. adrienne maree brown, website, accessed August 7, 2020, http:// adriennemareebrown.net.

2. SWNS Media Group, "Americans Check Their Phones 80 Times a Day," *New York Post*, November 8, 2017, https://nypost.com/2017 /11/08/americans-check-their-phones-80-times-a-day-study/.

3. Center for Humane Technology, website, accessed August 7, 2020, www.humanetech.com.

4. James Williams, Time Well Spent, "On Why and How to End the Attention Economy," TNW Conference, 2017.

5. Ezra Klein, *Why We're Polarized* (New York: Avid Reader Press, 2020).

6. K. Schaeffer, "Far More Americans See 'Very Strong' Partisan Conflicts Now Than in the Last Two Presidential Election Years," May 31, 2020, www.pewresearch.org/fact-tank/2020/03/04/far-more -americans-see-very-strong-partisan-conflicts-now-than-in-the-last -two-presidential-election-years.

7. CTZNWELL.org, accessed August 7, 2020, www.ctznwell.org.

8. Kerri Kelly, TedxBend, "The Privilege of Wellbeing," 2016.

9. Tim Adams, "How Freud Got under Our Skin," *The Guardian*, March 10, 2002, www.theguardian.com/education/2002/mar/10/medical science.highereducation.

10. D. Kahneman and A. Deaton, "High Income Improves Evaluation of Life but Not Emotional Well-Being," *Proceedings of the National Academy of Sciences* 107, no. 38 (2010): 16489–93, https://doi.org/10 .1073/pnas.1011492107.

11. Mary Watkins and Helene Shulman, *Toward Psychologies of Liberation* (New York: Palgrave Macmillan, 2008), 27.

12. Ibid., 149.

13. Mia Mingus, "Dreaming Accountability," *Leaving Evidence* (blog), May 5, 2019, https://leavingevidence.wordpress.com/2019/05/05 /dreaming-accountability-dreaming-a-returning-to-ourselves-and -each-other/.

14. Donna Hicks, *Dignity: Its Essential Role in Resolving Conflict* (New Haven: Yale University Press, 2013), 4.

15. John Paul Lederach, *The Little Book of Conflict Transformation* (Intercourse, PA: Good Books, 2003), 18.

16. HealingDialogueandAction.org, website, accessed August 7, 2020, http://healingdialogueandaction.org.

Chapter 10. Self-Reflection and Action

1. Cornel West, speech at Howard University, April 2011.

2. bell hooks, *Outlaw Culture: Resisting Representation* (London: Routledge, Taylor & Francis Group, 2015).

3. Joanna Macy and Chris Johnstone, *Active Hope: How to Face the Mess We're in without Going Crazy* (Warriewood, New South Wales: Finch Publishing, 2012), 3.

4. Joanna Macy, *World as Lover, World as Self: A Guide to Living Fully in Turbulent Times* (Berkeley, CA: Parallax Press, 2007), 141.

5. Ibid., 143–47.

6. Ibid., 146.

7. Tessa Hicks Peterson, *Student Development and Social Justice: Critical Learning, Radical Healing, and Community Engagement* (Springer International Publishing, 2018), 37.

SELECTED BIBLIOGRAPHY

Clare, Eli. *Brilliant Imperfection: Grappling with Cure*. Durham, NC: Duke University Press, 2017.

Corn, Seane. *Revolution of the Soul*. Boulder, CO: Sounds True, 2019.

Dalai Lama and Desmond Tutu. *Book of Joy: Lasting Happiness in a Changing World*. New York: Avery, 2016.

DeGruy, Joy. *Post Traumatic Slave Syndrome: America's Legacy of Enduring Injury and Healing*. Portland, OR: Joy DeGruy Publications, 2018.

Drake, Teo. "Vibrancy on the Margins: AIDS, Solidarity, and Justice." *Roots Grow the Tree* (blog), December 2, 2015. https://rootsgrowthetree.com/2015/12/02/vibrancy-on-the-margins.

Epstein, Mark. *The Trauma of Everyday Life*. New York: Penguin Books, 2014.

Fisher, Andy. *Radical Ecopsychology: Psychology in the Service of Life*. Albany: State University of New York Press, 2013.

Freire, Paulo. *Pedagogy of the Oppressed*. New York: Bloomsbury Academic, 2018.

Gendlin, Eugene T. *Focusing*. New York: Bantam Books, 2001.

Grossman, Warren. *To Be Healed by the Earth*. New York: Seven Stories, 2007.

Haga, Kazu. *Healing Resistance: A Radically Different Response to Harm*. Berkeley, CA: Parallax Press, 2020.

Haidt, Jonathan. *The Happiness Hypothesis: Finding Modern Truth in Ancient Wisdom.* New York: Basic Books, 2006.

Hanson, Rick. *Buddha's Brain: The Practical Neuroscience of Happiness, Love & Wisdom.* With Richard Mendius. Oakland, CA: New Harbinger Publications, 2009.

Hari, Johann. *Lost Connections: Uncovering the Real Causes of Depression—and the Unexpected Solutions.* New York: Bloomsbury, 2018.

Hendrix, Harville, and Helen Hunt. *Getting the Love You Want: A Guide for Couples.* New York: St. Martins Griffin, 2019.

Hicks, Donna. *Dignity: Its Essential Role in Resolving Conflict.* New Haven, CT: Yale University Press, 2013.

Hicks Peterson, Tessa. *Student Development and Social Justice: Critical Learning, Radical Healing, and Community Engagement.* Springer International, 2018.

hooks, bell. *Outlaw Culture: Resisting Representations.* New York: Routledge, 2015.

Klein, Ezra. *Why We're Polarized.* New York: Avid Reader Press, 2020.

Kornfield, Jack. *After the Ecstasy, the Laundry: How the Heart Grows Wise on the Spiritual Path.* New York: Bantam Books, 2001.

Lederach, John Paul. *The Little Book of Conflict Transformation.* Intercourse, PA: Good Books, 2003.

Levine, Peter A. *Healing Trauma: A Pioneering Program for Restoring the Wisdom of Your Body.* Boulder, CO: Sounds True, 2008.

———.*Waking the Tiger: Healing Trauma; The Innate Capacity to Transform Overwhelming Experiences.* Berkeley, CA: North Atlantic Books, 1997.

Macy, Joanna, and Chris Johnstone. *Active Hope: How to Face the Mess We're in without Going Crazy.* Warriewood, New South Wales: Finch Publishing, 2012.

Macy, Joanna. *World as Lover, World as Self: Courage for Global Justice and Ecological Renewal.* Berkeley, CA: Parallax Press, 2007.

McGonigal, Kelly. *The Upside of Stress: Why Stress Is Good for You, and How to Get Good at It.* New York: Avery, 2016.

Mingus, Mia. "Dreaming Accountability." *Leaving Evidence* (blog), May 5, 2019. https://leavingevidence.wordpress.com/2019/05/05/dreaming-accountability-dreaming-a-returning-to-ourselves-and-each-other.

Mooney, Jonathan. *Normal Sucks: How to Live, Learn, and Thrive Outside the Lines*. New York: Henry Holt and Company, 2020.

Newport, Cal. *Digital Minimalism: Choosing a Focused Life in a Noisy World*. New York: Portfolio, 2019.

Stevenson, Bryan. *Just Mercy: A Story of Justice and Redemption*. Melbourne: Scribe, 2016.

van der Kolk, Bessel. *The Body Keeps the Score: Mind, Brain, and Body in the Transformation of Trauma*. London: Penguin Books, 2015.

Watkins, Mary, and Helene Shulman. *Toward Psychologies of Liberation*. New York: Palgrave MacMillan, 2008.

INDEX

ABOUT THE AUTHOR

HALA KHOURI, MA, SEP, E-RYT, is a sought-after speaker and trainer on the subject of anxiety, trauma, building resilience, and social justice. She has been teaching yoga and movement for over twenty-five years and has been doing clinical work and trainings for fifteen years. Originally from Beirut, Lebanon, she has dedicated her life to the study of trauma, justice, and building resilience. She earned her BA in psychology from Columbia University and an MA in counseling psychology and an MA in community psychology from Pacifica Graduate Institute. Hala is trained in Somatic Experiencing, a body-based psychotherapy that helps resolve trauma and its symptoms.

Hala is a cofounder of Off the Mat, Into the World, a training organization that bridges yoga and activism within a social justice framework. She leads trauma-informed yoga trainings nationally and trains direct service providers and educators to be trauma informed and culturally responsive. She leads a monthly, online membership program called Radical Wellbeing. She lives in Venice, California, with her husband and two sons where she also teaches public yoga classes weekly.

www.halakhouri.com